First Family

FIRST FAMILY

George Washington

AND HIS

Intimate Relations

MIRIAM ANNE BOURNE

W · W · NORTON & COMPANY · NEW YORK · LONDON

COPYRIGHT © 1982 BY MIRIAM ANNE BOURNE
Published simultaneously in Canada by George J. McLeod Limited,
Toronto.
Printed in the United States of America
All Rights Reserved
First Edition

The text of this book is composed in photocomposition Baskerville, with
display type set in Goudy Old Style and Snell Roundhand. Composition
and manufacturing are by the Maple-Vail Book Manufacturing Group.
Book and binding design by Antonina Krass.

Library of Congress Cataloging in Publication Data

Bourne, Miriam Anne.
First family: George Washington and his intimate relations.
Bibliography: p.
Includes index.
1. Washington, George, 1732–1799—Family.
2. Presidents—United States—Biography.   I. Title.
E312.19.B68   1982   973.4′1′0922 [B]   81–18981
ISBN 0–393–01531–9   AACR2

W. W. Norton & Company, Inc. 500 Fifth Avenue, New York, N.Y. 10110
W. W. Norton & Company Ltd., 37 Great Russell Street,
London WC1B 3NU

1 2 3 4 5 6 7 8 9 0

FOR RUSTY
AND OUR FAMILY

Contents

III

THE YEARS BETWEEN (*1783–1789*)

IV

THE PRESIDENCY (*1789–1797*)

V

RETIREMENT (*1797–1799*)

Illustrations appear following page 123

INTRODUCTION

George Washington's family has seemed to most biographers a separate entity—moderately interesting from time to time, but not essential to an understanding of the great man himself.

As with most human beings, however, the Father of Our Country's relations with his relations were a vital part of his nature, profoundly affecting his character, personality, disposition, reactions, opinions, prejudices, and decisions. Washington's voluminous correspondence reveals the continuous interaction between the public man and the family man. Precise orders to a general after a battle or retreat are followed by an emotional letter to a brother which expresses the commander-in-chief's feelings about that event. Stern instructions to a secretary of state regarding the French are preceded by admonitions to stepson, nephew, or grandson to study harder.

An uneasy awareness of the needs of his mother, Mary, the tranquil presence of his wife, Martha, amusement at the high-jinks of resident granddaughter Nelly Custis intermingle with General and President Washington's official thoughts and actions, just as the grasses, swallows, and butterflies of his Mount Vernon fields blend with and respond to one another. And Mount Vernon, Virginia, is where the story of George Washington and his family begins and ends.

All of the research for *First Family* was done at the Mount Vernon reference library. The GW quotations come from the thirty-nine published volumes of his writings and the several volumes of his diaries. The library owns a substantial number of the original letters of a domestic nature—most of them in George Washington's own handwriting. (Contemporary copies of his official correspondence are preserved in letter books at the Library of Congress.)

Quotations from Washington family members were found in the Mount Vernon Library's extensive manuscript collection (originals and copies), in subject-matter notebooks, and in reminiscences and journals of people of the time, especially step-grandson George Washington Parke Custis's *Recollections and Private Memoirs of Washington* and tutor/secretary Tobias Lear's *Letters and Recollections of George Washington.* Although the quotes from these major sources are on file, they are not individually cited in *First Family* for fear of overwhelming the reader. Those from other books are footnoted, however. All are listed in the Bibliography.

Every writer who is interested in George Washington the public figure is indebted to his primary biographers Douglas S. Freeman and James T. Flexner. Elswyth Thane has written sensitively of Washington the farmer, and about several members of his family.

Occasionally, my reaction to family correspondence differs from that of previous biographers. In reading letters from stepson Jacky Custis or mother Mary Washington, for example, I have tried to see troublesome situations through their eyes as well as George's. And I take indignant exception to slighting references to Mary and Martha Washington's poor spelling and punctuation. For twentieth-century biographers to patronize eighteenth-century women on educational grounds is as rude as it is unfair. Besides, George made mistakes too; they make him seem like a real person.

The language of many of the letters is rich with George's and his family's personalities. "I cannot help thinking also that our Brother Charles is acting the part of a madman. . . . In God's name how did my Brothr. Saml. contrive to get himself so enormously in debt?" exclaimed George.

"I must entreat you" to visit my wife, he wrote a brother-in-law on departing for Cambridge to command the colonial troops. "I have no expection of returning till winter and feel great uneasiness at her lonesome situation."

"If you do not write, I will not write to you again," Martha Washington penned her son Jacky and daughter-in-law Nelly.

"Your letters come like drops of rain from a cloud in a dry season," Nelly told Tobias Lear, former tutor of two of her children who lived with their grandparents in the presidential household. "It gives me unfeined satisfaction to be informed my good Mamma . . . has at last seen the necessity of making the Dr. children respect as well as love her, for that they never would have done had she continued her former improper indulgence to them."

Did the president and commander in chief condone such indulgence in his own home? Washington would not insist on disciplining young grandson Wash, Lear explained. He says that "Mrs. Washington's happiness is bound up in the boy . . . any rigidity used toward him would perhaps be productive of Grevious effects on her."

His grandfather did write Wash some strict advice while he was away at college.

"Good God, how just your letter!" replied the penitent scholar.

You can see what intrigued me—the "Father of His Country" was a father indeed. Read on!

ACKNOWLEDGMENTS

To my friends on the Mount Vernon staff I am grateful for cheerful assistance and a consistently warm welcome. Special thanks are given to John Castellani, Ellen McCallister, and John Rhodehamel for sharing with me their quiet delight in the discovery of a man and his family through the written records they left behind.

George Washington's Intimate Relations*

WIFE	Martha Dandridge Custis
FATHER	Augustine
MOTHER	Mary Ball
HALF-BROTHERS	Lawrence *m.* Anne Fairfax (Mount Vernon, Fairfax Co.)
	Augustine (Austin) *m.* Anne Aylett (Wakefield, Westmoreland Co.)
BROTHERS	Samuel *m.* five times (Harewood, Berkeley Co.)
	John Augustine *m.* Hannah Bushrod (Bushfield, Westmoreland Co.)
	Charles *m.* Mildred Thornton (Happy Retreat, Berkeley Co.)
SISTER	Betty *m.* Fielding Lewis (Millbank; now Kenmore, Fredericksburg)
UNCLE	Joseph Ball
NEPHEWS & NIECES	Lawrence's children; died young
	Austin's children: William Augustine, Elizabeth [Spotswood], Jane [Thornton], Ann [Ashton]
	Betty's children: stepson John Lewis, sons Fielding, George, Lawrence, Robert, & Howell; daughter Betty [Carter]
	Samuel's children: sons Thornton, Ferdinand, George Steptoe, & Lawrence; daughter Harriot [Parks]
	John's children: sons Bushrod, Corbin, Augustine; daughters Jane [Washington] (*m.* Austin's son) & Mildred

*those that appear in *First Family*

	Charles's children: sons George Augustine & Samuel; daughters Frances [Ball] & Mildred [Hammond]
GRAND-NEPHEWS & NIECE	Fanny Bassett & George Augustine Washington's Maria, George Fayette, & Charles Augustine
STEPDAUGHTER	Martha (Patsy) Parke Custis
STEPSON	John (Jacky) Parke Custis
DAUGHTER-IN-LAW	Eleanor (Nelly) Calvert Custis Stuart
STEP-GRAND-CHILDREN	Elizabeth (Betsey) Parke Custis (m. Thomas Law), Martha (Patty) Parke Custis (m. Thomas Peter), Eleanor (Nelly) Parke Custis (m. Lawrence Lewis) & George Washington Parke Custis
STEP-GREAT-GRANDCHILDREN	Patty & Thomas Peter's two daughters and one son, Betsey & Thomas Law's daughter, Nelly & Lawrence Lewis's daughter
COUSINS	Lund Washington m. Elizabeth Foote (Hayfield, Fairfax Co.)
	Warner Washington m. Hannah Fairfax (Fairfield, Frederick Co.)
MARTHA'S SISTERS	Anne (Nancy) Dandridge m. Burwell Bassett (Eltham, New Kent)
	Elizabeth (Betsy) Dandridge m. John Aylett, Leonard Henley
MARTHA'S BROTHERS	William Dandridge, Bartholomew Dandridge
MARTHA'S NIECES & NEPHEWS	Frances (Fanny) Bassett m. GW's nephew George Augustine Washington; Burwell Bassett, Jr., & other Bassetts; John & Bart Dandridge, Patty Dandridge, etc.; Fanny Henley, etc.
MARTHA'S UNCLE	Francis Dandridge
OTHERS	Tobias Lear m. Mary (Polly) Long; son Benjamin Lincoln Lear
	m. Fanny Bassett Washington
	David Stuart m. Eleanor (Nelly) Calvert Custis

I

EARLY YEARS

1732–1775

"An Agreeable Consort for Life"

*M*ajor George Washington's orders to his Mount Vernon overseer were explicit: "I expect to be up to Morrow. . . . You must have the House very well cleand, and were you to make Fires in the Rooms below it w'd Air them. You must get two of the best Bedsteads put up, one in the Hall Room, and the other in the little dining Room that use to be, and have Beds made on them against we come. You must also get out the Chairs and Tables, and have them very well rubd and Cleand; the Stair case ought also to be polished in order to make it look well."

Did the bridegroom of three months fear Mount Vernon would not suit his new wife, or was Washington's lifelong attention to detail revealing itself? The twenty-seven-year-old, recently retired veteran of the French and Indian Wars had married Martha Dandridge Custis, a wealthy widow with two small children on January 6, 1759. After a "honey moon" spent at her plantation, White House, and in nearby Williamsburg, Virginia, the new family was to dwell at George's plantation, Mount Vernon, on the Potomac, a two-day journey from Martha's home territory and relatives.

Martha's reaction to the move can only be guessed. Surviving records do not bother to describe her personality until her second husband was famous. The only correspondence of the period are some no-nonsense business letters in Martha's writing concerning her deceased first husband's tobacco crop.

George's own mood is a subject for endless speculation. The fall before their marriage when he and Martha were engaged, George wrote letters to his married neighbor Sally Fairfax, which can at best be called ambiguous. Certain biographers assumed those letters were written to Martha; others described their status as "unsettled." A more realistic appraisal points unmistakably to a lingering infatuation with Sally: " 'Tis true, I profess myself a votary of love. I acknowledge that a lady is in the case, and further I confess that this lady is known to you . . . one who is too sensible of her charms to deny the Power whose influence he feels and must ever submit to. I feel the force of her amiable beauties in the recollection of a thousand tender passages. . . . You have drawn me, dear Madame, or rather I have drawn myself, into an honest confession of a simple Fact. Misconstrue not my meaning; doubt it not, nor expose it. The world has no business to know the object of my Love, declared in this manner to you, when I want to conceal it."

But a year later, a happily married George Washington was writing an acquaintance, "I am now I believe fixd at this Seat with an agreable Consort for Life and hope to find more happiness in retirement than I ever experienced amidst a wide and bustling World."

George's diaries indicate one surprising, personal detail, however—early and frequent social exchanges with Sally Fairfax and her husband.

January 20, 1760—Visited at Belvoir to day.
February 5   —Colo. Fairfax, his Lady . . . dined here.

February 6   —Colo. Fairfax and Mrs. Fairfax . . . dined
                 here.

On New Year's Day Washington had visited the farms on
his plantation. Arriving home he "found Mrs. Washington
. . . broke out with Meazles." Several days later: "Mrs.
Washington seem. to be very ill wrote to Mr. Green this
afternoon desiring his Company to visit her in the Morng."
The next day: "Mrs. Washington appeard to be something
better. Mr. Green however came to see her at 11 o clock
and in an hour Mrs. Fairfax arrivd."

Mrs. Fairfax? Of all people. Martha was no fool. Surely
Sally would not have been welcome at her sickbed had not
George's ardor by now been transferred to his wife. A clue
to the speedy turnabout may come from Benedict Arnold's
alleged testimonial to General Howe concerning the gratification of marriage to the newly wed: "Be assured, sir, no
sensations can have a comparison with those arising from
the reciprocity of concern and mutual felicity existing
between a lady of sensibility and a fond husband. I myself
had enjoyed a tolerable share of the dissipated joys of life,
as well as the scenes of sensual gratification incident to a
man of nervous constitution, but, when set in comparison
with those I have since felt and still enjoy, I consider the
time of celibacy in some measure misspent."[1]

During the 1760s, while the French and Indians were
being "well Drubd" without him, Washington busied himself with managing his own plantations and the estates of
wife and stepchildren. The family's agreeable presence is
detected in orders to London:

"A Childs Fiddle A Coach and 6 in a box
A Stable w' 6 horses 6 little books
for Childn begg. to Read

"1 Tester Bedstead 7½' pitch, with fashionable bleu or
bleu & White Curtains to suit a Roman lind w't the Ireld.
paper-Window Curtains of the same Bed Coverlid to match

1. James T. Flexner, *Traitor and Spy* (Boston, 1953), pp. 316–317.

4 Chair bottoms of the same . . . in order to make the whole furniture of this Room uniformly handsome and genteel.

"Sattin Ribbon, A Salmon-coloured Tabby . . . with Sattin Flowers . . . Ruffles, to be made of Brussels Lace . . . 6 lb. perfumd Powder."

Glimmers of restlessness do break through the domestic tranquility. Washington speaks of "the longing desire, which for many years I have had of visiting the great Matrapolis of that Kingdom [England] . . . but, I am now tied by the Leg and must set Inclination aside." Life at Mount Vernon was not perfect. "The Oyster Man still continuing his Disorderly behaviour at my Landing, I was obliged in the most preemptory manner to order him and his comp. away, which he did not Incline to obey till next morning." There was an indictment "against Jno. Ballendine for a fraud in some Iron he sold me." And "Doctr. Laurie came here. I may add Drunk."

Martha came down with whooping cough in 1761. "I have had it so bad that I could not go out of the house," she wrote her sister. "Carring children with so troublesome a disorder is a nussance." That summer a sick George's health was "in a very declining way." A trip to the warm springs in Berkeley County did nothing for his health or disposition. There were "about 200 people . . . full of all manner of diseases and complaints. I expect nothing from the air."

The childlessness of their union must have distressed George and Martha. (Although biographers have speculated about the cause, the record proves nothing.)

Yet, the overall impression during the first decade of the Washingtons' marriage is of a lively, self-satisfied pair, completely engaged in life. Mrs. Washington "inspected everything daily, giving out with her own hands the meals, going into dairy, the cellar, etc. . . . Then there was the garden in which Mrs. Washington took particular interest." Washington saw to the shearing of sheep, the grafting of fruit trees, the threshing and cleaning of wheat, the fishing for herring. There was time for entertainment—balls, boat races, a purse race at Accotinck, and theatrical performances. "[I with] Mrs. Washington & ye two childn. went up to Alexandria to see the Inconstant, or Way to Win him Acted. . . . Stayd in Town all day and saw the Tragedy of Douglas Playd." In writing to her sister, Martha spoke happily of the "Mirth and gaietys"[2] of Fairfax County.

Public duties were not allowed to become a burden— Washington attended only half the meetings of the vestrymen of Truro Parish, sat occasionally in the court at Alexandria. Legislative office beckoned. "Went to the Election of Burgesses for this County and was there, with Colo. West, chosen." Washington attended meetings of the Virginia Assembly for fifteen years and served on important committees. But during the time at Williamsburg his diary entries reflect mostly social occasions: "Came up to Colo. Bassett's to Dinner [Martha's sister Nancy and brother-in-law Burwell] . . . went to the Play . . . went a fox hunting . . . a draggdg for Sturgeon . . . a shooting and hair huntg. Dined . . . with Lord Botetourt (ye Govr.) and many other Gentlemen."

Life back home seemed more essential. Puppies were born—"Tarter, Jupiter, Trueman, and Tipler (being Dogs), and Truelove, June, Dutchess, and Lady, being the bitches." Farming methods were discussed—"We have been curiously entertained of late with the description of an Engine lately constructed (I believe in Switzerland) for taking up Trees by the Roots. . . ." Wheat was destroyed by rust. Indian corn and tobacco were "lost in Weeds and Grass [from] excessive Rains." The latest fashions were indulged in—"Mrs. Washington would take it as a favour if you woud . . . send her a fashionable Summer Cloak and Hatt . . . a grave and Handsome winter Silk (But not Yellow) . . . Red and Purple Gloves of French Kid."

In time, news of outside events penetrated the self-absorbtion at Mount Vernon. The Indian "Barbarities" on the frontier were "Melancholy to behold." Britain's 1765 Stamp Act hit the pocketbook, prompting a letter to Fran-

2. Original letter in Pennsylvania Historical Society, Dreer Collection.

cis Dandridge, Martha's London uncle. The Stamp Act
"engrosses the conversation." People "look upon this
unconstitutional method of Taxation as a direful attack
upon their Liberties." It would lessen America's purchases
from England, Washington warned his uncle-in-law. "Many
luxuries . . . can well be dispensd with . . . will introduce
frugality and a necessary stimulation to Industry."

No more raisins, almonds, anchovies, and tea? No more
"from the best House in Madeira a Pipe of the best Old
Wine, and let it be Secur'd from Pilferers"? No more "Sun-
dry Small Ornaments for chimny pieces"? A reduction in
the family standard of living would certainly be called for.

"My wife is very well," George concluded his letter to
Uncle Dandrige. She and the children "all join in making a
tender of their Duty and best respects to yourself and the
Aunt. . . . [We are] many Miles distant from any of my Wifes
Relations," he added compassionately, "who we seldom see
more than once a year."

Martha's letters to her sisters and brothers and nieces
always show a close relationship. George's letters to her
brothers and brother-in-law are equally familiar, even
jocular. "At all times I shall be glad to see you at this place
. . . my Love to Mrs. Bassett and the little ones," George
wrote Burwell Bassett. "I was favoured with your Epistle
wrote on a certain 25th of July when you ought to have
been at Church, praying as becomes every good Christian
Man who has as much to answer for as you have . . . could
you but behold with what religious zeal I hye me to Church
on every Lords day, it would do your heart good."

"YR. MOST DUTIFUL AND OBEDT. SON ... YOUR LOVING BROTHER"

*G*eorge's relationships with his own family were more complex. When he was three, father Augustine and mother Mary had moved their family from Pope's Creek in Westmoreland County north to Little Hunting Creek, later Mount Vernon, in Fairfax County. Augustine is believed to have built the central portion of the house. Seventeen-year-old half-brother Lawrence and fifteen-year-old half-brother Austin were at school in England, so George was the oldest child at home. When he was seven, the growing family moved south again to Ferry Farm opposite Fredericksburg, Virginia.

Washington's father owned three plantations and mills, was the manager and co-owner of six iron furnaces in Maryland and Virginia. He had been educated in England and took business trips to the mother country during his adult life. Augustine was a vestryman, a trustee of Fredericksburg, and high sheriff of Westmoreland County. George remembered him as tall, fair, well-proportioned, and fond of children. Although George was eleven or twelve when his father died, it is inconceivable that such an energetic man would not have had some influence on his best-known son. Mary was not the only parent.

What a romp historians have had with the mother of Washington! Nineteenth-century sentimentality created a virtuous myth; twentieth-century revisionism has created a nagging monster.

In 1720 thirteen-year-old Mary Ball had been orphaned. She was left with land, riding horses, saddle, maid, some jewels, household equipment, and a strong will.

Widowed at thirty-six in 1743, with five children between the ages of five and eleven (and two stepsons in their twenties), Mary Ball Washington was again called upon to be self-reliant—as self-reliant as an eighteenth-century woman could be. Augustine in customary fashion for the time had left his wife "the liberty of working my land at Bridge Creek Quarter for five years." Then the farm was to go to George. It was not until 1771 however, that Mary actually relinquished care of the property and moved to a small house in Fredericksburg near her daughter. She was compelled to rely on the generosity of her children, especially of George, until her death.

Mary would never be meek. A contemporary of George's relates his childhood memory of Mrs. Washington: "I was often there with George, his playmate, schoolmate, and young man's companion. Of the mother I was ten times more afraid than I ever was of my own parents. She awed me in the midst of her kindness, for she was, indeed, truly kind. I have often been present with her sons, proper tall fellows too, and we were all as mute as mice; and even now, when time has whitened my locks, and I am the grandparent of a second generation, I could not behold that remarkable woman without feelings it is impossible to describe. Whoever has seen that awe-inspiring air and manner so characteristic in the Father of his Country, will remember the matron as she appeared when the presiding genius of her well-ordered household, commanding and being obeyed."

At fourteen George expressed a desire to go to sea. Not surprisingly, Mrs. Washington objected strenuously. She sought the advice of a "loving brother" Joseph Ball, who supported her veto. At nineteen however, George took his ocean voyage.

Half-brother Lawrence's cough had always worried the family. "I heartily wish you may succeed in everything you have prospect of, but more especially in your Health, which shall always be the Prayer of your most Affece. Brothr," George's half-brother Austin wrote Lawrence in 1749. Lawrence's 1740–42 naval campaign in the West Indies as an officer under Admiral Edward Vernon had not been successful. Neither was subsequent treatment for his chronic cough.

As the oldest of seven children, Lawrence had heavy responsibilities when their father Augustine, died. He seems to have seen that half-brother George was instructed in geometrical and surveying exercises. (George made a survey of his brother's turnip field when he was fifteen.) Despairing of a cure for his ill health in America, Lawrence left wife Anne and infant daughter Sarah in September, 1751, for a visit to sunny Barbados. Nineteen-year-old George accompanied him.

"Early this morning came Dr. Hilary, an eminent physician recommended by Major Clarke, to pass his opinion on my brother's disorder, which he did in a favorable light, giving great assurance that it was not so fixed that a cure might be eventually made," George wrote in his diary November 2. "After Dinner was the greatest Collection of Fruits I have yet seen on the Table." "Avagado pair" and "Pine Apple" were especially noted. "Was treated with a play ticket to see the Tragedy of George Barnwell acted"— the beginning, perhaps, of George Washington's lifelong attachment to the theater. The "prospects were beautiful" overlooking Carlisle Bay.

Lawrence was less enthusiastic. "I own no place can please me without a change of seasons. We soon tire of the same prospect. Our bodies are too much relaxed—We have no kind of bodily diversions but dancing."

November 17 George "was strongly attacked with the small Pox: sent for Dr. Lanahan whose attendance was very constant till my recovery." Poor Lawrence did not recover his health in Barbados. December 22 George "took my leave of my brother." He returned home and Lawrence set sail for Bermuda. He asked George to bring Anne to him if his health improved. Sadly, it did not, and Lawrence returned home to die at thirty-four. Home was Mount Vernon (named for Lawrence's admiral). George leased the plantation from Anne two years later and inherited it when she died in 1761.

Soon after Lawrence's death twenty-year-old George applied for and was given his half-brother's position as an adjutant of the Virginia militia. A year later he volunteered for a dangerous mission. He carried a British demand to the French commander near Lake Erie that the French withdraw from their forts or be driven off "by force of arms."[3] The commander politely but firmly refused. So in his twenty-second year George found himself fighting (and losing to) the French.

He spent the winter of 1754–55 at Mount Vernon, but in June he and his militia regiment joined British regulars under General Edward Braddock to try again to defeat the enemy.

Mary Washington was horrified. She appeared at Mount Vernon and pleaded with George to change his mind. In vain. The son was as stubborn as she was. Undoubtedly, he recognized the need to be independent. But his mother cannot be blamed for believing him irresponsible in once again walking out to danger on four younger, fatherless siblings.

"Yr. mother and family are well and send their Several

3. James T. Flexner, *George Washington* I, (Boston, 1965), p. 54.

Greetings, desiring often to know of Yr. Welfare and Progress," wrote a mutual friend to George after he had departed with General Braddock.

His letters home were stiff and on the defensive. "I am, Honour'd Madam, Yr. most Dutiful and Obedt. Son. . . . I . . . am sorry it is not in my power to provide you with either a Dutch man [as a farmer], or the Butter as you desire. . . . I was sorry it was not in my power to call upon you as I went to, or came from Williamsburg to'ther Day."

At George's first engagement with the French the year before he knew he had made the right decision to enlist. "I hear the bullets whistle, and, believe me," he had written a brother, "there is something charming in the sound." After the humiliating defeat at the forks of the Ohio (now Pittsburgh) and General Braddock's death, the bullets were less romantic. George felt it necessary to set the record straight for his mother. The setback appeared in "a worse light . . . than it deserves." The Virginia troops had been brave. The English troops "behav'd with more cowardice than it is possible to conceive." He sought a little sympathy: "I luckily escap'd with't a wound, tho I had four Bullets through my Coat, and two Horses shot under me." George had taken charge, the only officer left; and he was "not half recover'd from a violent illness." No wonder his mother thought he should have stayed at home.

George could not leave his position at Fort Cumberland in western Maryland until September. "So that I shall not have the pleasure of seeing you till then, unless it be in Fairfax." A month later he wrote again. "If it is in my power to avoid going to the Ohio . . . , I shall. But if the Command is press'd upon me by the gen'l voice of the Country, & offer'd upon such terms as can't be objected against, it wou'd reflect eternal dishounour upon me to refuse it; and that, I am sure must, or ought, to give you greater cause of uneasiness than my going in an honourable Com'd."

There was "no end to my Troble while George was in the army," Mary said when it was all over three years later, "butt he has now given it up." Her son wrote later in his diary: "Returnd in the Evening to Mother's—all alone with her."

George's letters during the French and Indian Wars to his brothers were as warm and open as those to his mother were reserved. "The pleasure of your Company at Mount Vernon always did, and always will, afford me infinite satisfaction," he wrote half-brother Austin. "As much hurried as I am at present, I can't think of leaving this place without writing to you," he told brother John. "As I have heard since my arriv'l at this place a circumstantial acct. of my death and dying speech, I take this early oppertunity of contradicting both and of assuring you that I now exist." They had been "most scandalously beaten by a trifling body of men."

To Austin George admitted what he would not tell his mother. ". . . our shameful defeat, which really was so scandalous that I hate to have it mention'd." Austin was quick to reassure him. "I am certain your character does not in the least suffer here, for I do assure you as far as I can inform myself (and I have taken great pains) you are in as great esteem as ever with the Govr. here and especially the house of Burgesses." Don't give up your commission, Austin begged. "You country never stood more in need of yr. assistance and we are all apprehensive if you give up." This time Uncle Joseph Ball sent a supportive letter: "It is a Sensible Pleasure to me to hear that you have behaved your-Self with such a Martial Spirit in all your Engagements with the French nigh Ohio. Go on as you have begun; and God prosper you. We have heard of General Braddock's Defeat Every Body Blames his Rash Conduct."

Austin died in 1762, making George the oldest of the family. Glimpsed in his writings and diaries are signs of a strong, ongoing relationship with his younger brothers. "I was in great hopes to have met with you at F[redericksburg] or seen you at this place on your way up, but it would almost seem as if you had foresworn this part of the Country," George wrote Sam in 1772 when Sam was moving to the western part of Virginia. News that Charles's mother-in-law feared George would take advantage of her daughter if Charles died before becoming of age, annoyed George. "If she believes I am capable of taking these ungenerous advantages [she] knows little of the principles which govern my conduct; however I suppose Mrs. T. is actuated by prudent motives. . . ." To Charles he sent his love.

Charles was useful for some things. In 1764 big brother George tried to unload on him a tenant he'd been pestered with—"a very honest man and very punctual in paying his Rents." From 1770 a somewhat shady letter is preserved which George might have preferred destroyed. The Proclamation of 1762 had given western lands to French and Indian War veterans. George was eager to add to his by buying bounty rights from other veterans: "As you are situated in a good place for seeing many of the Officers at different times, I should be glad if you woud (in a joking way, rather than in earnest at first) see what value they seem to set upon their Lands. . . . If you should make any purchases, let it be done in your name, for reasons I shall give you when we meet. . . . In the whole of your transactions, either with the Officers, or on this other matter; do not let it be known that I have any concern therein. . . . Show no part of this Letter, so that you can be drawn into no trouble or difficulty in the Affair."

Charles sometimes caused concern. "I cannot help thinking also that our Brother Charles is acting the part of a madman, to rent his land to people of such force who must, in the nature of things cut down and destroy his land to all intents and purposes," George wrote Sam in 1771.

But generally, there are comfortable references to his siblings: "Went to Fredericksburg with my Brother Sam, who I found there . . . was disappointed of seeing my Sister Lewis. Dind and lodg at my Brother's. . . . Cattle bought at My Bro. John Washington's Sale . . . guest, inc. my Brother Charles came here . . . shooting together." For a few glorious days in the spring of 1768 all the brothers got together at Sam's along with their brother-in-law and a cousin.

Sister Betty was two years younger—"the most majestic and imposing female I ever beheld," wrote a grand-nephew. She ressembled her mother and brother George. Assuming she would marry, her father had left her a mere £400 and two Negroes. Fortunately, she did. Colonel Fielding Lewis built her a handsome house in Fredericksburg and impregnated her with a passel of children. Betty's Mill-bank* made for George a congenial lodging place between Mount Vernon and Williamsburg. Mother was nearby—but not too near.

Historians call John Augustine Washington's favorite brother. During the French and Indian campaigns John and his bride, Hannah Bushrod, managed Mount Vernon. Their devoted service and friendship was so appreciated that years later Washington willed his home to their oldest son Bushrod.

*later called Kenmore.

"Our Dear Patsy Custis"

$\mathcal{M}$artha Washington was a mother of a different sort than her mother-in-law. Her two children, Jacky and Patsy Custis, were fussed over and indulged. Orders went to England for: "Tea Sett . . . Toys . . . A Bird on Bellows . . . A Cuckoo . . . A Turnabout Parrot . . . A Grocers Shop . . . A Neat dressed Wax Baby . . . An Aviary, Prussian Dragoon . . . A Man Smoakg. A stifned Coat made of fash. Silk, 6 handsome Egrets different sorts . . . 1 pr. little Scissors . . . 1 Fash. dressd Doll . . . A Box Ginger br'd Toys and Sugr. Imags. and Comfits."

In 1761 Mr. Walter Magowan was hired as a tutor to drum a little learning into Jacky's and Patsy's eight- and six-year-old heads. He promptly overwhelmed them with a diet of "2 Copies of the Rudimt. of the Latin F, 2 Phaedrus Fables, 2 Salust, Horace, the Gram'l Exercises, Erasmus, Latin & Eng'h Dic'y."

John Stedlar, a local music teacher, gave spinet lessons

on a new spinet to Patsy and violin lessons to Jacky. Martha had a few spinet lessons too. A 1759 songbook has her name in it in Washington's writing.

Martha was reluctantly persuaded to leave Jacky behind on a visit to one of George's brothers in 1762 and regretted every minute of it. "I carried my little patt [Patsy] with me," she wrote sister Nancy Bassett, "and left Jackey at home for a trial to see how well I could stay without him. though we ware gan but qon fortnight I was quite impatient to get home. If I at aney time heard the doggs barke or a noise out, I thought thair was a person sent for me. I often fancied he was sick or some accident had happened to him so that I think it is impossible for me to leave him as long as Mr. Washington must stay when he comes down."

Martha had good reason to fret over her daughter. June 14, 1768, when Patsy was twelve, a poignant entry appeared in Washington's diary: "Sent for Doctr. Rumney to Patsy Custis who was seized with fitts." Eight months later: "Joshua Evans, who came here last Night, put an Iron Ring upon Patcy (for Fits) and went away after Breakfast." (Iron was thought to have curative powers.)

The epilepsy which afflicted Patsy haunted the household: "We set out to go to Captn. McCarty's, but Patcy being taken with a fit on the Road by the Mill, we turnd back. . . . Mrs. Washington requests the favour of you to get her 2 oz. Spirit of Ether . . . in Annapolis, for Miss Custis . . . mecicinal brew . . . capsules of musk . . . purging, bleeding . . . fit drops, aether . . . a vial of nervous drops . . . powders . . . package of valerian." Poor Patsy.

"We are all in the usual way, no alteration for the better or worse in Patcy," Washington wrote his brother-in-law Burwell Bassett, in June, 1769. In August the family journeyed hopefully to Warm Springs. Washington recorded the trip in his diary.

August 6—Arriv'd at the Springs about One oclock.
      19—Rid with Mrs. Washington and others to the

Cacapehon Mountain to see the prospect from thence.
>20—Went to church in the fore and afternoon.
>23—Dined alone—Patcy unwell.

"Many poor, miserable objects" were fellow visitors, Washington wrote. "Patsy is troubled with a complaint . . . little benefit as yet."

Although it is almost impossible to catch a glimmer of Patsy's personality from remaining records, her way of life can be discerned. In many respects Patsy's adolescence was typical for her time and station. Every spring and fall in the late 1760s she accompanied her mother and stepfather to the Virginia Assembly sessions, visiting relatives along the way and staying with the Bassetts at Eltham in New Kent County near Williamsburg.

In May of 1769 the governor dissolved the House of Burgesses because of its impudent "Virginia Resolves." Undaunted, the Burgesses passed a nonimportation agreement. The Washingtons had left Williamsburg by the time of the ball where the ladies wore homespun to demonstrate their support.

In December George and his family were back. "Mrs. Washington and children, myself, Colo. Bassett, Mrs. Bassett and Betsey Bassett all Eat Oysters at Mrs. Campbell's abt. one oclock, and afterwards went up to Eltham," he recorded in his diary. The family had ridden to Williamsburg in a new green chariot with gold trim.

At home Patsy visited neighbors, practiced "Psalms and Hymns set for the Spinnet," went to balls and the theater in Alexandria, sat for a miniature by C. W. Peale. She and her friend Milly Posey,* joined "the Scholars" in Mr. Christian's dancing class, which met sometimes at Mount Vernon. Soon after breakfast instruction began. One dancing master of the time was "punctual and rigid in his discipline, so strict indeed that he struck two of the young Misses for

---

*Milly may have lived at Mount Vernon for awhile.

a fault in the course of their performance, even in the presence of the Mother of one of them!"[4]

From England Washington ordered "A handse. Suit of Brussels Lace for a young lady . . . a Garnet comb for the Hair . . . to Suit a Sett of Necklace & Earrings . . . A Tambour Frame to Work Muslin in with proper needles and Thread . . . A String of Amber Beeds . . . Quadrille [a Spanish game] Counters made of Mother of Pearle . . . Fordices Sermon's, A Large Family Bible bound in Morrocco with Cuts, and Silver Clasps . . . A small and very neat Prayer Book . . . Ladys Magazine."

But a foreboding tone permeates the diary references to Patsy—"Docter Rumney came. . . . Dr. John Johnson paid for Miss Custis." And always the medicine—"fit drops . . . 2 Bottles Norris's Drops . . . Mrs. Washington begs the favour of you to get her, for Patcy, another Phial of aether."

Once on the way home from Williamsburg in the fall, Patsy was detained for nine days at Ferry Farm near Fredericksburg with epilepsy, ague, and fever. "A small Phial to be frequently smelt to . . ." wrote Dr. Johnson the following March, "to prevent faitiness . . . a small bottle of ointment . . . decoction taken if occasion requires it tho' I hope Nature will perform her office without . . . regular moderate exercises . . . keep Body cool and open . . . by use of Barley Water & light cooling Food."

"The family not sicklier than common," Washington wrote his brother-in-law during a comparatively good period. But seventeen-year-old Patsy's poor health affected all. Martha feared to have Jacky travel abroad. "The unhappy situation of her daughter," Washington wrote Jacky's school master when the idea was being discussed, "has in some degree fixed her eyes upon him as her only hope."

In April, 1773 fifteen-year-old Betsey Bassett died. George wrote his brother-in-law a letter of condolence. He

4. Philip V. Fithian, *Journal and Letters, 1767–1774* (Princeton, 1900), pp. 63–64.

spoke with compassion of "Mrs. Bassett, whose loss and feelings are much to be pitied." But he recommended "cheerful acquiescence to the Divine Will . . . the ways of Providence being inscrutable, and the justice of it not to be scanned by the shallow eye of humanity."

Two months later he was not so sanguine when writing the Bassetts. June 20, 1773: "It is an easier matter to conceive, than to describe the distress of this Family; especially that of the unhappy Parent of our Dear Patsy Custis, when I inform you that yesterday removd the Sweet Innocent Girl Entered into a more happy and peaceful abode than any she has met with in the afflicted Path she hitherto has trod.

"She rose from Dinner about four o'clock in better health and spirits than she appeared to have been in for some time; soon after which she was seiced with one of her usual Fits, and expired in it, in less than two minutes without uttering a word, a groan, or scarce a sigh. This sudden, and unexpected blow, I scarce need add has almost reduced my poor Wife to the lowest ebb of Misery; which is encreas'd by the absence of her son, (whom I have just fixed at the College in New York from whence I returned the 8th Inst) and want of the balmy consolation of her Relations; which leads me more than ever to wish she could see them."

Washington's diary entry is succinct but just as moving: "At home all day. About five o'clock poor Patcy Custis Died Suddenly."

A careful look at the close-mouthed entries which follow reveal a grieving household. Friends and relatives came and went doing what little they could. "Colo. Fairfax and Lady . . . dined here, Patcy Custis being buried. . . . My Brother John and Family. . . ." George attempted to comfort Martha by distracting her. "I continued at home all day. . . . Went with Mrs. Washington and Dind at Belvoir. . . . Rid with Mrs. Washington to the Ferry Plantn. . . . Rid with Mrs. Washington to Muddy hole, Doeg Run, and Mill Plantations. . . . Mrs. Washington and self went to Belvoir to see them take Shipping."

A letter from Sister Betty's husband, Fielding Lewis, typified attitudes of friends and family, but probably did little to ease Martha's grief: "Poor Patsys death must have distressed Mrs. Washington very much, but when she considers the unhappy situation she was in and the little probability of ever getting well, she must conclude that it's better as is. . . ."

Rings and other mourning trinkets were ordered. Eleanor Calvert, Jacky's young fiancée, arrived. She stayed on until her family came to fetch her, substituting as best she could for the lost daughter.

From King's College (Columbia) in New York Jacky sent his mother and stepfather an amazing pair of letters. The one to George began as an academic report card: "I attend at stated Hours, the Professors in Mathematicks, Languages, Moral and experimental Philosophy [I] hope the Progress I make . . . will redown not only to my own credit, but to the credit of those who have been instrumental in placeing me here."

A gray horse had been disposed of. Not until the third paragraph does Jacky speak of Patsy: "I myself could not withstand the Shock, but like a Woman gave myself up entirely to melancholy for several days . . . my mind was . . . illy capable to give others what, it stood so much in need of itself."

Would a trip to New York help his bereaved mother?— "for everything at Mount Vernon must put her in mind of her late Loss. . . . I beg you to write me immediately . . . as I am extremely anxious to hear how my mother bears this misfortune and of your own health."

When Jacky's letter to "My dear Mamma" arrived, Martha must have devoured it. He began by telling her of his well-being. His studies were going well. He dined with the professors and "am look'd upon in a particular Light by them all." His "apartments" and daily routine were described. Again, it was not until the third paragraph that Jacky could bring himself to mention "my dear only Sister's death. . . . My nature could not bear the Shock, but sunk under the load of oppression." He and his servant Joe were in deep mourning.

Self-centered. Spoiled. Immature. Yet Jacky was probably right. He would comfort his mother best by reassuring her about himself, by sharing her profound grief, and by offering advice such as his stepfather gave: "Remember you are a Christian and that we ought to submit with Patience to the divine Will. . . . [Patsy] deserves Grace [She] enjoys the Bliss prepar'd only for the good and virtuous." Patsy—his "well beloved Sister."

"A Boy of Good Genius"

*H*ow soon one wonders, did the young Custis heir comprehend that the generous inheritance from his dead father entitled him to pleasure? From the beginning his stepfather was careful to see that his orders to England for Jacky and Patsy were charged to their accounts. A copy of the marriage certificate went immediately to Robt. Cary & Co., Merchants, London, as proof that Washington was now legally entitled to one-third of Daniel Parke Custis's estate for himself and Martha, and was the custodian of the remaining two-thirds for his minor stepchildren.

While Washington ordered "handsome but plain Cloathes . . . for myself . . . neither Lace nor Embroidery," he specified livery—perhaps at Martha's direction—for eight-year-old Jacky's servant "suited to the Arms of the Custis family." At fourteen Jacky was "tolerably well grown" and sported a "Silver lacd Hatt . . . two Strong Pocket knives and one Handsome fowling piece." At eighteen social life in Annapolis demanded "best blew Bever Coating, Wash'd Inda Waistts. one with gold the other with Silvr. Sprigs, if they be in taste."

Jacky was encouraged in the gentlemanly arts of fiddle-playing and fox hunting. It was probably Washington's idea to order "Case Surveyors Plottg Instruments" for him. A member of the landed gentry should learn to survey his own lands, Washington believed. In 1768 Martha was persuaded to send Jacky away to the school in Caroline County (later in Annapolis, Maryland) of the Reverend Jonathan Boucher. An affectionate letter from his stepfather preceded him. Jacky was: "a boy of good genius, about 14 yrs. of age, untainted in his morals, and of innocent manners. Two yrs and upwards he has been reading of Virgil, and was (at the time Mr. Magowan left him) entered upon a Greek Testament, tho I presume he has grown not a little rusty in both, having had no benefit of his Tutor since Christmas. . . . If he comes, he will have a boy . . . and two Horses, to furnish him with the means of getting to Church and elsewhere as you may permit; for he will be put entirely and absolutely under your tuition, and direction to manage as you think proper in all respects. [Jacky is] a promising boy; the last of his Family and will possess a very large Fortune; add to this my anxiety to make him fit for more useful purposes, than a horse Racer."

Letters to and from Boucher about Jacky continued for several years and reveal Washington as a father and husband with whom one can easily sympathize. July 31, 1768, George Washington to Jonathan Boucher: Washington is sending some missing books. If the pain in Jacky's stomach should return "with any other Symptoms of worms," Dr. Mercer should be called for.

"We should be very glad to hear how he is reconciled to an absence from home, unusual to him 'til now. . . . It has been a matter of some concern to me . . . least you should conceive that by asking your particular care of . . . Mr. Custis, I meant to bespeak any peculiar Indulgence . . . on the contrary, as he is healthy, and of good constitution, I rather wished that he might lead a life of as little Indulgence and dissipation as should be thought necessary to relax, and keep his spirits in their full strength and vigour; [He should be] restrain'd from the practice of those follies & vices which youth, & inexperience, are but too naturally led into the commission of. . . . I may have ask'd too much—the sollicitude of every Parent havg prompted them, I suppose, to make the same request."

Boucher didn't mind. His primary concern was the boy's welfare. August 2, 1768, Jonathan Boucher to George Washington: "Mastr Custis is a Boy of so exceedingly mild and meek a Temper, that I meant no more by my Fears, than a Doubt that possibly he might be made uneasy by ye rougher manners of some of his School fellows. I am pleas'd however, to find that He seems to be perfectly easy and happy in his new Situation. . . . I have not seen a youth that I think promises fairer to be a good and useful man than John Custis! 'Tis true, he is far of being a brilliant Genius . . ."—or a devoted student.

September 4, 1768, George Washington to Jonathan Boucher: Jacky had a fever and vomitted while in Westmoreland, "which induced his Mamma to take him home with us, 'til he is perfectly restored."

January 26, 1769, George Washington to Jonathan Boucher: "After so long a vaction, we hope Jacky will apply close to his Studies, and retrieve the hours he has lost from his Book since your opening School, he promises to do so, and I hope he will."

July 27, 1769, George Washington to Jonathan Boucher: "I have further to desire, at the request of Mrs. Washington, that you will restrain Jacky from going too frequently into the water, or staying too long in it."

October 14, 1769, George Washington to Jonathan Boucher: "Jack's stay has been longer here than we intended but we hope he will endeavor to make atonemt. by extry. diligence."

Fall, 1769, Jonathan Boucher to George Washington:

"You will remrmy how I complain'd of Jack's Laziness, which, however, I now hope is not incurable."

February 3, 1770, George Washington to Jonathan Boucher: "The uncertainty of your return from Maryland (as we heard that Potomack was Froze below Cedar Point) added to the difficulty, and indeed the danger of crossing the Waters between this and your House are the Reasons of Jacky's detention here so long."

August 30, 1770, Jacky Custis to George Washington: "I have nothing new to tell you. . . . My love to Mama and sister . . . with the greatest respect. Yr. Obedt. Son."

By now Washington was exasperated with his stepson. December 6, 1770, George Washington to Jonathan Boucher: "His mind is a good deal released from Study, and more than ever turnd to Dogs Horses and Guns; indeed upon Dress and equipage. . . . I must beg the favor of you, therefore, to keep him close to those useful branches of Learning which he ought now to be acquainted with, and as much as possible under your own Eye. . . . The time of Life he is now advancing into requires the most friendly aid and Council (especially in such a place as Annapolis); otherwise, the warmth of his own Passions, assisted by the bad example of other Youth, may prompt him to actions derogatory of Virtue." Washington wants his stepson under Boucher's own roof . . . "nor allow him to be rambling about of Nights in Company with those, who do not care how debauched and viceous his Conduct may be."

Boucher was irritated with Jacky, too. December, 1770, Jonathan Boucher to George Washington: "Probably, ere long, you will find out that He has lost his Watch; and He deserves to be severely reprimanded for his Carelessness. I have the Watch, but do not care soon to put Him out of Pain.

Were all Those who have the Care and Direction of children as attentive to their real Interests, We shou'd not have so many complaints of Children spoil'd by Parental Indulgence . . Your Sentim't of this young Gentleman have for some Time been my own I must confess to You I never did in my Life know a youth so exceedingly indolent, or so surprisingly voluptuous: one wd suppose nature had intended Him for some Asiatic Prince."

The new year began inauspiciously. January 2, 1771, George Washington to Jonathan Boucher: Jack's return has been delayed while he pursued his "favourite amusement of Hunting. . . . He returns now he says, with a determination of applying close to his Studies."

February 3, 1771, George Washington to Jonathan Boucher: "[It] never was my Intention that Jacky shou'd be restrained from proper Company; to prevent as much as possible his connecting with Store boys, and that kind of low loose company who wou'd not be displeas'd at the debauchery of his Manners, but perhaps endeavor to avail themselves of some advantages from it, is all I had in view."

While Martha agonized over Patsy's poor health, her husband shielded her from knowledge of a potential danger for Jacky. April 20, 1771, George Washington to Jonathan Boucher: Washington had given Boucher permission for Jacky to go to Baltimore to be innoculated against smallpox. He was keeping Mrs. Washington "in total ignorance of his having been there, til I hear of his return, or perfect recovery." He asks Boucher to write him "under cover of Lund Washington, and in a hand not your own . . . her anxiety and uneasiness is great. . . . Indeed, I believe, was she to come to the knowledge of his being at Baltimore (under Innoculation) it wou'd put an infallible stop to her journey to Williamsburg and possibly delay mine." Washington will immediately visit Jacky if there is any danger, he assures Boucher. He defends his deceit: Mrs. Washington "having often wish'd that Jack wou'd take and go through the disorder without her knowing of it; that she might escape those Tortures which Suspence w'd throw her into."

May 2, 1771, Jonathan Boucher to George Washington: "Jack is out of all danger," Boucher assures Washington. But he is "exceedingly displeased with Mr. Custis, that, according to my express Desire to Him, He is not Here [at

Annapolis] Himself, to write to put both Yourself and his Mother out of all further Anxiety on his account." Jacky had stayed in Baltimore for a wedding.

By this time Washington wondered if Boucher was doing all he could for Jacky's education. June 5, 1771, George Washington to Jonathan Boucher: "Jacky is again late in returning to school. He has to wait 'till his cloaths could be washd & got in readiness." Washington fears his progress in classical knowledge is "trifling." He is not "much [farther] in Latten than when he left Mr. Magowan, knows [little] Arithmetick, and is quite ignorant of the Gr[eek] Language. . . . [Jacky] has filled me with a sincere concern, not because of the expence . . . but on acct. of the lost time."

July 4, 1771, Jonathan Boucher to George Washington: "I am much concern'd at your apprehensions of Mr. Custis's slender Improvements . . . tho' not equal to what they might have been, are, I believe, not inferior to Those of any other young man so circumstanced. . . . He is not, indeed as you observe, much farther advanced than under Mr. Magowan."

The young man himself had a partial explanation. August 18, 1771, Jacky Custis to George Washington: "I am exceedingly thankful for your Remarks on my letters. . . . I am obliged to own, that I am one of those who put off every thing to the last. And how it should or does happen, I know not, but so it is. . . ."

When Boucher suggested a trip abroad to "perfect" Jacky's education, Washington fretted over the question of authorizing the expenditure. Guardians "are to consider in what light their conduct may be viewed by those whom the constitution hath placed as a controlling power over them; because a faupas committed by them often incurs the severest centure, and sometimes punishment; when the intention may be strictly laudable," he wrote. Jacky's estate was not profitable. "Every farthing which is expended in behalf of this gentleman, must undergo the inspection of the General Court." Fearing criticism, Washington consulted his stepson's relatives for their opinions. "[I] conceive there is much greater circumspection to [be observed] by a Guardian than a natural Parent."

Friends and relatives were generally against the proposed trip, some "on acct. of expence," others "as being almost the last of a Family, think he should run no risks that are to be avoided." Washington thought Jacky should enlarge his mind, but did not want to appear to be promoting the trip. His mother says that "he is lukewarm in the scheme . . . (if . . . not speak[ing] her own sentiments rather than his). . . . If it appeared to be his inclination to undertake this tour, and it should be adjudged for his benefit, she would not oppose it, whatever pangs it might give her to part with him. This declaration she still adheres to, but in so faint a manner, that I think, what with her fears and his indifference, it will soon be declared that he has no inclination to go."

It did seem time, however, to think of sending Jacky somewhere else. Washington discussed the matter with Dr. Witherspoon, president of the college at Princeton, New Jersey, and a Presbyterian. (Boucher was Church of England.) Boucher's reaction sputtered to Mount Vernon. November 19, 1771, Jonathan Boucher to George Washington: "Dr. Witherspoon, it seems, said I *ought* to have put Him into Greek. . . . Had Dr. Witherspoon examined this young Gentleman, he would not, indeed, have found Him possess'd of much of that dry, useless and disgusting School-boy kind of Learning; but . . . not illy accomplished . . . in that liberal, manly and necessary knowledge befitting a Gentleman.

"If . . . you resolve on removing Him, all I have to add is a Request, that it may not be to Princeton . . . your own college [William and Mary at Williamsburg] is a better one. . . . If, however, the Objections to W be insuperable, I wou'd then recommend New-York."

A year later Washington wrote Boucher (January 7, 1773): "From the best enquiries I could make whilst I was in and about Williamsburg, I cannot think William & Mary College a desirable place to send Jack Custis to; the Inattention of the Masters, added to the number of Hollidays, is the Subject of general complaint; and affords no pleasing prospect to a youth who has a good deal to attain, and but a short while to do it in. (As there no longer seems to be any thoughts of his crossing the Atlantic) I have I think, determined to send him to the Philadelphia College; which . . . stands equally fair with any other, and being nearer, is more agreeable to his Mother."

January, 1773, Jonathan Boucher to George Washington: "It is certainly expedient to remove Mr. Custis to some Place of publick Education and speedily," Boucher agrees, but he still recommends New York. Dr. Cooper the President, is "a correspondent and a countryman."

Just how expedient it was to remove Mr. Custis, Boucher did not suspect. The eighteen-year-old boy had fallen in love with sixteen-year-old Eleanor (Nelly) Calvert, one of ten children of Benedict Calvert of Mount Airy, across the Potomac from Mount Vernon in Maryland. Washington wrote to Nelly's father: "I am now set down to write you on a Subject of Importance, and of no small embarrassment to me." Miss Nelly has "amiable qualifications." But Jacky's "youth, inexperience, and unripened Education, is, and will be insuperable obstacles in my eye, to the completion of the Marriage." It is "not that I have any doubt of the warmth of his Affections, nor . . . any fears of a change in them; but at present, I do not conceive that he is capable of bestowing that due attention to the Important Consequences of a marriage State, which is necessary to be done by those, who are Inclin'd to enter into it; and of course, am unwilling he should do it till he is." Washington wants the couple to wait. "If the Affection which they have avowed for each other is fixd upon a Solid Basis, it will receive no diminution in the course of two or three years." He is not "desirous of breaking off the Match," Washington assures his neighbor, only of postponing it. Jacky "consider[s] himself as much engaged to your Daughter as if the indissoluble Knot was tied." He will "stick close to his Studies . . . avoid those little Flirtations with other Girls which may, by dividing the Attention, contribute not a little to divide the Affection."

Benedict Calvert replied: "I should be dead to Parental feelings, wher I untouched with the polite manner in which you are pleased to compliment Nelly's Qualifications. . . . I intirely agree with you, that it is, as yet, too early in life for Mr. Custis to enter upon the matrimonial State [and] hope with you, that separation will delay, not break off the match."

Jonathan Boucher was flabbergasted but supportive. "I hardly remember ever to have been more surpris'd, than I was a few days ago, on being informed by the Governor of the Engagement that had taken Place between Mr. Custis and Miss Nelly Calvert. . . . You will remember, I always thought, that He was enamoured of Miss Betsey [Calvert]. . . . It gives Me great uneasiness to learn . . . that you think me, in some measure to blame. . . . Miss Nelly Calvert has merit enough to fix Him, if any Woman can. . . . I know her well and can truly say, she is all that the Fondest Parent can wish for a darling child."

Early in May Washington escorted Jacky to the college in New York. (Jonathan Boucher had had his way.) On the way home he stopped to visit two of his sister's sons at Princeton. A little over a month later came the tragic news of Patsy's death. "The shock was severe," Dr. Cooper wrote Washington of Jacky's reaction. "He has already gained much upon ye affections of his Instructors."

In September Dr. Cooper sent Jacky home on vacation with a note sure to please his stepfather. "Dr. Cooper presents his most respectful comps to Col. Washington, and *returns* him his Son in Law, without any Vices that he knows of, and with many Virtues, wherewith he is perfectly acquainted." A letter from a professor was even more enthusiastic. Jacky "has with . . . constancy devoted himself to his Studies . . . his Affability and Courtesy have enderd him to mine, as well as to the Affection of all who are concern'd on his Education."

But waiting at home was Nelly Calvert. December 15,

1773 Washington sent a chagrined letter to Dr. Cooper. "The favourable account you was pleas'd to transmit me of Mr. Custis's conduct at College, gave me very great satisfaction; and I hope to have felt an increase in it by his continuance at that place . . . but these hopes are at an end; and at length, I have yielded contrary to my judgment, and much against my wishes to his quitting College; in order that he may enter soon into a new scene of Life, which I think he would be much fitter for some years hence, than now; but having his own inclination, the desires of his mother and the acquiessence of almost all his relatives, to encounter, I did not care, as he is the last of the family, to push my opposition too far; and therefore have submitted to a Kind of necessity."

Dr. Cooper replied graciously, "The Professors much lament Mr. Custis's unexpected Departure." But "I cannot but think [from all Jacky had told him about Nelly] that they bid very fair for Happiness." To Jacky himself went sentiments both affectionate and admiring. "I assure you of my being very sensibly affected upon your leaving this College. The Regard I had conceived for you, from the Regularity of your Conduct and the Goodness of your Disposition, could not possibly produce any other Effect upon me."

Washington's diary, February 3, 1774: "Set out after an early dinner (with Lund Washington) for Mr. Calvert's to Mr. Custis's Wedding, who was this Eveng. married to Miss Nelly Calvert." Martha, who was still in mourning for Patsy, stayed home at Mount Vernon.

Soon afterward Jacky Custis addressed his stepfather. February 20, 1774, Jacky Custis to George Washington: "How to express fully my Thankfulness for the many kind Offers you have lately made Nelly and myself; I find great Loss of Words; and shall endeavor by my future Behavior and Actions to testify the sincere and just Regard I entertain of them. Nelly joins me in Love to Mama and yourself."

II

THE WAR

1775–1783

"REPEAL OF THE STAMP ACT OUGHT TO BE REJOICED AT"

*T*he mature woman admiringly described by later acquaintances hardly resembles the timorous and overprotective Martha Washington glimpsed during the prewar years.

February 3, 1771—"Mrs. Washington may accompany me to my Brothers."

February 20, 1771—"Mrs. Washington has given over the thoughts of accompanying me to Frederick."

May 21, 1772—Washington doubts "whether Mrs. Washington stretches as far as Annapolis."

Yet for eight years this same middle-aged woman would make an arduous, annual trek from Mount Vernon to the uncomfortable places her husband had camped the Revolutionary army for the winter. Their names resound with her stamina and love:

Cambridge

Morristown

Valley Forge
Middlebrook
Morristown
New Windsor
Newburgh
Rocky Hill

Martha probably did not see the Revolution coming until it was upon her. In '66 she may have felt with George that "Repeal of the Stamp Act . . . ought much to be rejoiced at." In '69 she heard the excitement when the governor of Virginia dissolved the House of Burgesses for asserting its right to tax, watched her husband meet with neighbor George Mason to draw up a list of British goods to boycott in protest over the Townshend Acts. Martha may have known of her husband's letter to Mason that same year: "At a time when our lordly masters in Great Britain will be satisfied with nothing less than the deprivation of American freedom . . . no man should scruple or hesitate a moment to use a-ms in defense of so valuable a blessing. . . ."

But a variety of interests engaged George Washington. From October to December of 1770 he took a two-hundred-fifty-mile trip with his friend Dr. Craik to inspect western lands promised by the Virginia government to French and Indian War veterans. In July, 1771 he left for Williamsburg with "both my head and my hands too full of [farm] business to allow more than a hasty ill-digested letter." A bill did pass that session which interested George intensely— "to raise money for the purpose of opening and extending the navigation of Potomack from the Tide Water to Fort Cumberland."

The spring '72 session otherwise was "tiresome and very unimportant." But in '73 Martha learned of George's vote for the significant intercolony Committee of Correspondence for mutual self-defense. In '74 he voted for a sympathetic day of fasting when the British closed the port of Boston after the Tea Party. Virginia daringly called for a

Continental Congress to meet in Philadelphia that fall; Washington was elected a delegate. He was definitely a junior member of the delegation—"an attentive observer and witness,"[5] he characterized himself. An observer once described Washington's low-keyed style during legislative sessions: "a modest man, but sensible, and speaks little in action, cool, like a bishop at his prayers."[6] Patrick Henry was predictably more impatient. He said his fellow Virginian's mind was "slow in operation, being little aided by invention or imagination, but sure in conclusion."[7]

5. Flexner, *George Washington* I, p. 325.
6. Ibid., p. 251.
7. Ibid., p. 316.

"An Honor I By No Means Aspired To"—1775

*I*n 1775 Washington's neighbors in a number of Virginia counties elected him a field officer in the militia. He got out his old uniform and drilled troops. In April came news of Concord and Lexington. When her husband had his uniform pressed and packed for the journey as a delegate to the Second Continental Congress in May, Martha knew she had reason to worry. The letter below could not have been entirely unexpected. Years later Martha burned most of her husband's letters to her. (Only a brief one of hers to him remains. "My Dearest," it begins. . . . "Your most affectionate Martha Washington.")[8] The two crucial letters written by George from Philadelphia in June, 1775, were found later by a granddaughter.

8. Original letter owned by Joseph Fields.

Philadelphia, June 18, 1775.[9]: "My Dearest: I am now set down to write you on a subject which fills me with inexpressible concern and this concern is greatly aggravated and increased, when I reflect upon the uneasiness I know it will cause you. It has been determined in Congress, that the whole army raised for the defence of the American cause shall be put under my care, and that it is necessary for me to proceed immediately to Boston to take upon me the command of it.

"You may believe me, my dear Patsy, when I assure you, in the most solemn manner that, so far from seeking this appointment, I have used every endeavor in my power to avoid it, not only from my unwillingness to part with you and the family, but from a consciousness of its being a trust too great for my capacity, and that I should enjoy more real happiness in one month with you at home, than I have the most distant prospect of finding abroad, if my stay were to be seven times seven years. But as it has been a kind of destiny, that has thrown me upon this service, I shall hope that my undertaking it is designed to answer some good purpose, You might, and I suppose did perceive, from the tenor of my letters, that I was apprehensive I could not avoid this appointment, without exposing my character to such censures, as would have reflected dishonor upon myself, and have given pain to my friends. This, I am sure, could not, and ought not, to be pleasing to you, and must have lessened me considerably in my own esteem. I shall rely, therefore, confidently on that Providence, which has heretofore preserved and been bountiful to me, not doubting but that I shall return safe to you in the fall. I shall feel no pain from the toil of the danger of the campaign; my unhappiness will flow from the uneasiness I know you will feel from being left alone. I therefore beg, that you will summon your whole fortitude, and pass your time as agreeably as possible. Nothing will give me so much sincere

9. Original letter owned by Armistead Peter, 3d. *Tudor Place* (Georgetown: Privately Printed, 1969), pp. 44–5.

satisfaction as to hear this, and to hear it from your own
pen.

"If it should be your desire to remove into Alexandria
(as you once mentioned upon an occasion of this sort) I am
quite pleased that you should put it into practice, and Lund
Washington may be directed by you to build a kitchen and
other houses there proper for your reception. If on the
other hand you should rather incline to spend a good part
of your time among your friends below, I wish you to do
so. In short my earnest and ardent desire is that you will
pursue any plan that is most likely to produce content, and
a tolerable degree of tranquility; as it must add greatly to
my uneasy feelings to hear that you are dissatisfied or complaining at what I really could not avoid.

"As life is always uncertain, and common prudence dic-
tates to every man the necessity of settling his temporal
concerns while it is in his power, and while the mind is calm
and undisturbed, I have, since I came to this place (for I
had not time to do it before I left home) got Colonel Pen-
dleton to draft a will for me, by the directions I gave him,
which will I now enclose. The provision made for you in
case of my death will, I hope, be agreeable: I have included
the money for which I sold my land (to Doctor Mercer) in
the sum given you as also all my other debts. What I owe
myself is very trifling, Cary's debt excepted, and this would
not have been much if the bank stock had been applied
without such difficulties as he made in the transference.

"I shall add nothing more at present as I have several
letters to write, but to desire that you will remember me to
Milly and all friends, and to assure you that I am, with the
most unfeigned regard. My dear Patcy, Yr affecte Go
Washington.

In an attempt to alleviate his wife's uneasiness, George
entreated their relatives to visit her. June 19, 1775, George
Washington to stepson Jacky Custis: ". . . My great concern
upon this occasion is, the thought of leaving your mother
under the uneasiness which I fear this affair will throw her
into; I therefore hope, expect, and indeed have no doubt,

of your using every means in your power to promote her quiet. I have, I must confess, very uneasy feelings on her account. . . ."

June 19, 1775, George Washington to brother-in-law Bassett: "It is an honour I by no means aspired to. It is an honour I wished to avoid, as well from an unwillingness to quit the peaceful enjoyment of my Family, as from a thorough conviction of my own Incapacity and want of experience in the conduct of so momentous a concern. . . . P. S. I must entreat you and Mrs. Bassett if possible to visit at Mount Vernon, as also my Wife's other friends. I could wish you to take her down, as I have no expectation of returning till Winter and feel great uneasiness at her lonesome situation."

June 20, 1775, George Washington to brother John Washington: "I am now to bid adieu to you, and every kind of domestick ease, for a while. I am Imbarked on a wide Ocean, boundless in its prospect, and from whence, perhaps, no safe harbour is to be found." Will his brother visit his wife and keep up her spirits?

June 23, 1775, George Washington to Martha Washington: "My dearest: As I am within a few minutes of leaving this City, I could not think of departing from it without dropping you a line; especially as I do not know whether it may be in my power to write again till I get to the camp in Boston—I go fully trusting in that Providence, which has been more bountiful to me that I deserve and in full confidence of a happy meeting with you sometime in the Fall— I have not time to add more as I am surrounded with Company to take leave of me—I retain an unalterable affection for you, which neither time or distance can change my best love to Jack & Nelly, and regard for the rest of the Family concludes me with the utmost truth & sincerety. Yr. entire G. Washington."

In July Washington wrote John from army headquarters

Phil.ª June 23.ᵈ 1775.

My dearest,

As I am within a few Mi
nutes of leaving this City, I could not
think of departing from it without
dropping you a line, especially as I
do not know whether it may be in
my power to write again till I get to
the Camp at Boston — I go fully trus
ting in that Providence, which has
been more bountiful to me than I de
serve, & in full confidence of a happy
meeting with you sometime in the
Fall — I have not time to add more as
I am surrounded with Company to
take leave of me — I retain an un
alterable affection for you, which
neither time or distance can change
my best love to Jack & Nelly, & regard
for the rest of the Family concludes
me with the utmost truth & sincerity
Yᵗ entire · G⁰
                                    G Washington

MOUNT VERNON LADIES' ASSOCIATION

in Cambridge, Massachusetts, describing the New England countryside and comparing it to Virginia. In the years ahead Washington's letters to his brothers, brothers-in-law, Jacky Custis, cousin Lund, and other relatives would reveal more of his opinions and emotions than all the official correspondence put together.

July 20, 1775, George Washington to brother Sam Washington: "I come to this place the 3d instant and found a numerous army of Provincials under very little command, discipline or order. I found an enemy who had drove our People from Bunker's Hill strongly Intrenching and from accts had reason to expect before this, another attack from them; but as we have been incessantly (Sundays not excepted) employed in throwing up works of defense, I rather begin to believe now that they think it rather a dangerous experiment and that we shall remain sometime watching the motions of each other, at the distance of little more than a mile and in full view."

Cousin Lund Washington had been entrusted with the care of Mount Vernon, and reported almost weekly to George throughout the war. August 20, 1775, George Washington to Lund Washington: "Spinning should go forward with all possible dispatch. . . . I would not have you buy a single bushel of Wheat till you can see with some kind of certainty what Market the Flour is to go to.

"I can hardly think that Lord Dunmore [Royal Governor] can act so low, and unmanly a part, as to think of siezing Mrs. Washington by way of revenge upon me; howev'r, as I suppose she is, before this time gone over to Mr. Calvert's, and will soon after retng., go down to New Kent, she will be out of his reach for 2 or 3 months to come, in which time matters may, and probably will take such a turn as to render her removal either absolutely necessary, or quite useless." The officers in this continental army, Washington complained to his cousin "are the most indifferent kind of People I ever saw."

Lund reassured George about Martha's safety: " 'Tis true that many people made a stir about Mrs. Washington continuing at Mount Vernon, but I cannot think her in any kind of danger. . . . She does not believe herself in danger . . . ten minutes notice would be sufficient for her to get out of the way." Lund added later, "She has often declared she would go to the camp if you would permit her."

As fall came, George continued to report to his family. September 10, 1775, George Washington to John Washington: ". . . we are well and in no fear or dread of the Enemy . . . Very securely Intrenched, and wishing for nothing more than to see the Enemy out of their strong holds, that the dispute may come to an Issue."

October 13, 1775, George Washington to John Washington: "I gladly learnt that your Family were recover'd of the two complaints which had seized many of them, and confined my Sister. . . . I am very glad to hear also that the convention had come to resolutions of arming the People . . . also pleased to find that the Manufactury of Arms and Ammunition have been attended to with so much care.

"I am obliged to you for your advice to My Wife, and for your Intention of visiting of her; seeing no great prospect of returning to my Family and Friends this Winter I have sent an Invitation to Mrs. Washington to come to me, altho. I fear the Season is too far advanced . . . to admit this with any tolerable degree of convenience." George has told his wife "of the difficulties [of] the journey and left it to her own choice."

November 26, 1775, George Washington to Lund Washington: "I observe you mention something in respect to the removal of my valuable Furniture, but where can you carry it? or what will be done with it. I have no doubt of your using every endeavor to prevent the destruction of My House . . . but I would have you run no hazards about it, unless an oppertunity presents of doing some damage to the Enemy." Washington is happy "to think that my business is in the hands of a person in whose integrity I have not a doubt, and on whose care I can rely." His cousin is to "Let the Hospitality of the House, with respects to the poor, be kept up; Let no one go hungry away."

Martha did accept her husband's invitation to visit him at headquarters. George Lewis, Betty's son, accompanied his aunt and her maid to Cambridge in late November. Jacky and Nelly Custis rode along too—he as Fairfax County's official bearer of funds for the troops.

When George had been made commander of the colonial troops, he had sent his chariot and horses back to Mount Vernon and ridden from Philadelphia to Cambridge with the other generals, aides, and servants by horse and phaeton. Martha and party now rode in the Washington chariot to army headquarters. A coachman and a postilion guided the four horses; Jacky's servant rode behind, leading still another horse.

It was a long way from Virginia to Massachusetts for a woman who had never been north of Alexandria, especially in winter. It took a week to get to Philadelphia where Martha was greeted with ceremony. "You have seen the figure our arrival made . . . in Philadelphia . . . proper and I left it in as great pomp as if I had been a very great somebody."[10] She was invited to a ball which was then canceled due to "these troubled times." The commander in chief's wife agreed with those who thought a ball in poor taste. "Their sentiments on this occasion were perfectly agreeable unto her own."[11]

After several days in Philadelphia Martha set out again. It took another week to reach chilly Massachusetts. Boston's Mercy Warren, who was capable of a tarter pen, described the southern newcomer approvingly. Mrs. Washington had received her "with that politeness and Respect shewn in a first interview among the well bread and with the Ease and Cordiality of Friendship of a much Earlier date. . . . the Complacency of her Manners speaks at once the Benevolence of her Heart, and her affability, Candor, and Gentleness Qualify her to soften the hours of

10. (Original letter in Morgan Library.) Douglas S. Freeman, *George Washington III*, (New York, 1951), p. 581.

11. Flexner, *George Washington II*, p. 59.

private Life, or to sweeten the Cares of the Hero and smooth the Rugged scenes of War."[12] Jacky was "a sensible Modest agreable young Man." Nelly had an "Engaging Disposition but of so Extrem Delicate a Constitution . . . a lind of Langour . . . prevents her being so sociable as some Ladies . . . a want of health a little Clouds her spirits."[13]

Martha quickly took the bachelor headquarters in hand and imposed her gracious stamp. "His lady is of a hospitable disposition, always good-humored and cheerful, and seems to be actuated by the same motives with himself, but she is rather of a more lively disposition. They are to all appearances a happy pair," recorded one Nicholas Cresswell in his journal.

Martha heard the shells and cannon and shuddered at the sound. Poor Boston and Charlestown. She tried to keep her fears to herself. It was beautiful country.

12. Freeman, *George Washington IV* (New York, 1957), p. 77.
13. *Adams Family Correspondence I,* (Cambridge, 1963), pp. 385–6.

"Absolved From All Allegiance To, or Dependence Upon, the Crown"—1776

*T*he early months of America's Independence year found the commander in chief somewhat relaxed. He appreciated the support he was getting from home, he assured his family. February 28, 1776, George Washington to Burwell Bassett: "I thank you heartily for the attention you have kindly paid to my landed affairs on the Ohio, my interest in which I shall be more careful of . . . as in the worst event they will Serve for an asylum. . . . Mrs. Washington says that she has wrote all the news she could get (and ladies you know are never at a loss) to Mrs. Bassett." A tragic piece of news was the drowning in January of Martha's and Nancy Bassett's brother William Dandridge.

The British occupying Boston reacted dramatically to the spectacular arrival of Henry Knox's cannon from captured Fort Ticonderoga in March, 1776. Martha Washington to Nancy Bassett: "A few days ago Gen. Clinton, with several companyes sailed out of Boston Harbor, to what place distant for, we cannot find out. Some think it is to Virginia he is gon others to New York. . . . If Gen. Clinton is gon to New York, Gen. Lee is there before him, and I hope will give him a very warm reception—."

Washington led the rest of the army south to defend New York. To John he sent a series of letters—a bizarre blend of "difficulties and distresses," domestic news, and historic events. March 31, 1776, George Washington to John Washington: "General Lee is the first Officer in Military knowledge and experience we have in the whole Army. He is zealously attach'd to the Cause, honest and well meaning, but rather fickle and violent I fear in his temper. . . . I am with every Sentiment of true Affection, your Loving Brother and faithful friend."

April 29, 1776, George Washington to John Washington from New York: "Thank you for your kind and frequent rembrance of me. . . . Mrs. Washington is still here, and talks of taking the Small Pox, but I doubt her resolution. Mr. and Mrs. Custis will set out in a few days for Maryland."

May 31, 1776, George Washington to John from Philadelphia: He is glad of the vote of the Virginia convention to propose to the Continental Congress "to declare the Colonies free and independent States, absolved from all allegiance to, or dependence upon, the Crown or Parliament of Great Britain. . . . Mrs. Washington is now under Innoculation. This is the 13th day and she has very few Pustules; she would have wrote to my Sister but thought it prudent not to do so . . . danger in conveying the Infection."

June 4, 1776, George Washington to Burwell Bassett: "Mrs. Washington got through the Fever and not more than about a dozen Pustules appearing." After she has recovered she will go to New York "if matters there are in such a situation as to make it a fit place for her to remain."

Jacky wrote his stepfather June 9 that he was glad "so dear a mother" had recovered from the smallpox innoculation. He spoke of Maryland's political situation—"the

People being discontented with their Convention; Mr. Calvert [Jacky's father-in-law] takes a part which I fear will involve Him in many troubles." Calvert was a member of Maryland's upper house, which was loyal to England. On June 10 Jacky wrote his stepfather again: "I am extremely desirous . . . to return you Thanks for your parental care which on all Occasions you have shewn me. . . . Few have experienced such care and attention from real parents as I have done. . . . I often wish'd to thank you personally, but my resolution fail'd me. . . . I thought I cou'd more strongly express my Gratitude in this manner . . . sincere regard and love I bear you."

By July 9 Washington had seen the Declaration of Independence which had been approved by the Continental Congress. He ordered the Declaration "Proclaimed before all the Army under my immediate command . . . the measure seemed to have their most hearty assent." Thirteen days later George had something else to write about. July 22, 1776, George Washington to John Washington from New York: "We have a powerful [British] Fleet within full view of us." Mrs. Washington is in Philadelphia with "thoughts of returning to Virginia."

August 20, 1776, Martha Washington to sister Nancy Bassett: "The Genl in New York informed me that Lord Dunmore with part of his fleet was come to General Howe at Staten Island, that another division of Hessians is expected before they think, the regulars will begen thare attack on us; some hear begen to think thare will be noe Battle after all—Last week our boats made another attempt on the ships up the north river—and had grapp a fire ship with the Phoenix ten muniets but she got cleare of her; and is come down the river on satterday last. Our people burnt one of the tenders. I thank God we shant want men—the army at New York is very large and numbers of men are still going there is at this time in the city, four thousand on the march to the camp and the Virginia is daily Expected. . . . I do, my dear Sister, most religiously wish there was an end to the war."

There was happy family news that month, however. From

Maryland Jacky wrote his mother that "Nelly was safely delivered of a fine daughter . . . a strapping Huzze . . . the other little one [which had miscarried] was a mere dwarf to this. . . . I wish you were present." Martha hurried home to see her first grandchild, as Washington led the army in battle against the British.

The subsequent behavior of his troops was "nothing to write home about." But Washington did. After the British attack and the humiliating American retreat from Long Island in September and during the months that followed, George's family served as a sympathetic vent for his anger and frustration and self-justification. To John from Harlem Heights he wrote that the retreat (from Long Island) had been "absolutely necessary. . . . The sick were numerous and an object of great Importance." At the time of the British landing troops were "running away in the most shameful and disgraceful manner." Washington tried to rally them, but they "ran off without firing a Single Gun. The Dependence which the Congress has placed upon the Militia . . . will totally ruin our Cause. . . . £50,000 should not induce me again to undergo what I have done."

To cousin Lund George wrote that the condition of the army "is not a fit one to be publicly known or discussed. . . . If the men will stand by me (which, by the by, I despair of), I am resolved not to be forced from this ground while I have life."

Thoughts of home consoled him. To Sam he asked: Would his brother convey his best wishes to his friends? ". . . neither time, distance, or change of Circumstances have, in the smallest degree altered the Affection I have ever entertained for them."

Another letter went to Sam on October 18. "We are, I expect, on the eve of something very important. . . . I will do the best I can." But by November 19 Harlem Heights had had to be evacuated, a skirmish at White Plains had ended in defeat, and Fort Washington had surrendered. Washington wrote John from Hackensac, New Jersey. "This is a most unfortunate affair, and has give me great Mortification. . . . It is a matter of great grief and surprize to me to find the different states so slow [in] levying their quota's of Men . . . my difficulties, and the constant perplexities and mortifications I constantly meet with, derived from the unhappy policy of short enlistments, and delaying them too long. . . . I am wearied almost to death with the retrograde Motions of things."

Three days later Fort Lee had to be abandoned to the enemy. Washington hurried the American army south, across New Jersey's meadows and marshes, with the British in pursuit.

December 10, 1776, George Washington to Lund Washington from the Falls of Delaware, South Side: "I wish to heaven it was in my power to give you a more favorable account of our situation than it is. . . . I tremble for Philadelphia. . . . [I have] no time . . . to send the Horses I promis'd. Mrs. Washington must therefore make the old grays serve her a little while longer."

December 17, 1776, George Washington to Lund Washington from ten miles above the Falls: ". . . we have prevented them from crossing; but how long we shall be able to do it God only knows, as they are still hovering about the river." General Lee has been captured. "Unhappy man! Taken by his own imprudence. [Lund should] have my papers in such a Situation as to remove at a short notice in case an Enemy's Fleet should come up the River . . . let them go . . . to my Brothers in Berkeley."

"A Variety of Difficulties and Perplexities"—1777

*H*ome in Virginia Martha and her family were sick with worry. After the crossing of the Delaware Christmas Eve and "the glorious victory at Trenton" Martha's brother Bartholomew Dandridge wrote George a congratulatory letter. But, he cautioned: "I cannot help mentioning the anxiety I have suffered from the critical situation you have been in for some time past . . . it is you alone that can defend us against our enemies I wish these considerations would caution you against exposing your Person too much I am sure you can have no Idea of your real value to us may all that is great and good attend you."

The general himself was more discouraged than alarmed. January 22 he wrote Jacky Custis. ". . . The misfortune of short enlistments, and an unhappy dependence upon militia have shown their baneful influence . . . if we could have got in the militia in time, or prevailed upon those troops whose times expired . . . to have continued . . . we might, I am persuaded, have cleared the Jerseys entirely of the enemy.

"I do not think that any officer since the creation ever had such a variety of difficulties and perplexities to encounter as I have. How we shall be able to rub along till the new army is raised, I know not. [Reported are] . . . the shocking wastes committed by Howe's army—their ravaging, plundering, and abuse of women. . . .

"It is painful to me to hear of such illiberal reflections upon the eastern troops as you say prevails in Virginia. I do not believe any of the states produce better men . . . but it is to be acknowledged that they are (generally speaking) most wretchedly officered . . . no people fly to arms readier than they do, or come better equipped. . . . My love to Nelly, and compliments to Mr. Calvert's family."

February 24, 1777, George Washington to John Washington: There are "frequent skirmishes . . . frequent Desertions . . . serves to waste their Army." Continental militia are "here today, and gone tomorrow; *whose ways, like the ways of Providence are, almost inscrutable. . . .* [John] must not communicate our weakness to any body. . . . My warmest Affections . . . strongest assurances of unalterable love to yourself."

In early March Washington was ill for ten days. Martha's decision to travel from Mount Vernon to Headquarters at Morristown, New Jersey, undoubtedly made him feel better. Soon other officers' wives, lady visitors, and riding parties enlivened headquarters and lifted spirits. March 15 Washington reported to his brother Sam. General Howe was expected to move toward Philadelphia. Thornton, Sam's oldest son, was with his uncle: "I got Thornton Innoculated on Wednesday Week . . . he is in a very fair way of having the disorder slightly. . . . I shall give him an Ensigncy. . . .

"I wish it had been in my power to have paid greater regard to your recommendation of Captn. Cooke and others . . . immersed as I am in business . . . and cautious of showing more civility to my own Countrymen [Virginians] than others to avoid the charge of partiality . . . best affections . . . to my Sister and the little ones."

April 5, 1777, George Washington to Samuel Washington: He is surprised that Howe had made no move except to Peekskill. "Our troops come in exceedingly slow . . . it looks to me as if we should never get an army assembled."

April 12, 1777, George Washington to John Washington: ". . . To my great surprize we are still in a calm . . . it seems next to impossible to make our Officers, in any of the States, exert themselves in bringing their Men to the Field, as if it was a matter of Moonshine whether they came to day, to morrow, a Week, or a Month hence. The Campaign will I expect, be opend without Men on our side."

In May Washington moved the army to Middlebrook, New Jersey, in anticipation of action at last. Martha again headed south. And George continued to report to family members on the war and to count on their letters to boost his morale.

June 1, 1777, George Washington to John Washington: George fancies Howe is expecting "foreign Mercenares. . . . I can no otherwise Acct. for Genl. Howes inactivity." During the British destruction of stores at Danbury, Connecticut, the enemy lost five hundred men. "We lost no Powder at all."

June 29, 1777, George Washington to John Washington: ". . . certain it is, I have not received a Letter from you for some considerable time.

". . . they [the British] are equal to Indians in concealing their loss, by a removal of their dead, and were they to take up the business of Scalping they would much resemble Savages, in every respects! . . . By means of their Shipping . . . they have it much in their power to lead us a very disagreeable dance."

During August Washington ordered his troops on the march in pursuit of the enemy. The soldiers felt "harrassed by Marching, and Counter Marching," George wrote John from Germantown, Pennsylvania. The same month Martha's brother Bartholomew Dandridge, reported to George: "a formidable fleet in [Chesapeake] Bay and poor defenses . . . my Sister Washington is in perfect Health, at Elthem. . . . Mr. Custis's little girl is recovering from the whooping cough."

Jacky Custis belatedly "with the most infeined pleasure congratulate you and your successes in the Jerseys over the enemy." He was sorry to bother the general with personal business, but wanted some land to rent. His stepfather replied from Perkiomy, Philadelphia City, in September: "It was always my intention, if agreeable to your mother to give you the offer of renting her Dower Estate in King William. . . . Leave the amount of rent to an impartial gentleman." But Washington wants "really and not Nominally to get what was intended as a Rent."

Martha, meanwhile, was back at Mount Vernon running a small-pox clinic for relatives. She had brought her Bassett nephews with her from Eltham. Their aunt sent them home with a letter to her sister. ". . . they have been exceeding good Boys indeed and I shall hope you will lett them come to see me when ever they can spare so much time from school. . . . The last Letter I had from the General . . . he says nothing hath happened since the unsuccessfull attack upon our forts on the Delawar. . . . Jack is just come over, he tells me that Little Bet is grown as fat as a pigg."

September 11 there was finally some real action between the armies. The battle at Brandywine that day was lost, although they had almost won a subsequent engagement, George wrote Sam. That was at Germantown, October 4. He described it for John: They had made a "Surprize" attack in "a thick Fog . . . upon the point (as it appeared to every body) of grasping a compleat Victory, our own Troops took fright and fled with precipitation and disorder. . . ." The loss was balanced by "the Important and glorious News" of Burgoyne's surrender at Saratoga on the Hudson. George has received John's "kind and Affectionate letters. . . . I very sincerely congratulate you on the change in your Family . . . [the union of] the young couple." Their uncle "wish[es] them joy."*

The enemy was now occupying Philadelphia. George wrote Sam October 27. ". . . we hovering round them, to distress and retard their operations as much as possible." George will speak to General Woodford about Thornton "without going out of the common line (which I know you would not wish me to do, and there by incur censure.)"

From "White Marsh, 12 Miles from Philadelphia" Washington wrote Jacky Custis on November 14, ". . . war expected every moment between France and Britain. God send it." To his sister-in-law Hannah (through John) he sent softer sentiments. "Thanking her for the nice and elegant stocking she was obliging enough to send me. . . . I shall set great store by them, and will wear them for her sake. . . . My love attends my sister, the young married couple, and the rest of your family."

---

*John's daughter Jane married half-brother Austin's son William.

"Extreme Fatigue and Hardship"—1778

*E*arly in the year when she made the trip north to winter headquarters at Valley Forge, Martha was badly in need of comforting. Sister Nancy Bassett, "the greatest favorite I had in the world," had died in December. In turn, George probably poured out his frustrations over Congress's tardiness in providing shoes, bread, blankets, and pay for the barefoot, frozen soldiers camped at Valley Forge, and his hurt over the "Conway cabal" which politicked unsuccessfully to replace him as commander in chief.

Yet, despite mutual turmoils, Martha once again brought a gracious atmosphere to the crowded headquarters in a rented farmhouse. There were quiet conversations over cups of tea with the wives of other officers, amateur theatrics in the bakehouse, singing around the fire in the evenings. The miserable conditions of the troops moved the women. They nursed sick soldiers and wielded their knitting needles in a vain attempt to warm an army's fingers and toes.

Jacky and Nelly had a new baby. Washington congratulated the father "upon the birth of another daughter, and Nelly's good health; and heartily wish the last may continue, and the other be a blessing to you." From Virginia cousin Lund reported, "the grandchildren are two beauties."

More supplies had arrived at Valley Forge by the time Martha wrote Mercy Warren March 7. "Officers and men are chiefly in Hutts, which they say are tolerable comfortable." The army is "as healthy as can well be expected. . . . I hope, and trust, that all the states will make a vigorous push early this spring, if everything can be prepared for it, and thereby putting a stop to British cruelties—and afford us that peace liberty and happyness which we have so long contended for."[14] To Jacky and Nelly Martha wrote petulantly but understandably: "If you do not write I will not write to you again." She sent "a pretty new doll for Bett . . . the general joins me in love to you both."

On April 30 came the glorious news of an alliance with France against Great Britain. The treaty was read aloud to the soldiers and greeted with cheers. In spite of the "extreme fatigue and hardship which the Soldiers underwent in the course of the Winter . . . want of Cloathe . . . Provisions . . . very sickly," the army was "in exceeding good spirits," George wrote John. In June the British evacuated Philadelphia. In anticipation of more fighting in the north, Martha left camp.

For a change, the American army was successful—at Monmouth, New Jersey, where "an unfortunate and bad beginning, turned out a glorious and happy day." General Washington's army followed the retreating British to New York State. Off the coast hovered a French fleet. From White Plains Washington happily sent Jacky his thanks for "your cordial and affectionate congratulations on our late

14. Original letter owned by Harvard College Library.

success at Monmouth, and the arrival of the French at the Hook . . . love to Nelly, Colonel Bassett and friends." In August Washington wrote Jacky that his intention to buy land and settle in Fairfax County would be "an agreeable measure to your Mother, and a *very* pleasing one to me." He was worried about the terms of purchase and in an uncharacteristically apologetic tone proffered advice about other land matters. Jack was assured of his stepfather's "Attachment, affection to you."

As yet, the alliance with France was unproductive. The "unfortunate Storm" in Rhode Island which had done such damage to the French fleet "blasted in one moment, the fairest hopes that ever were conceived," George complained to John from New York State in September. He sent congratulations on the birth of his brother's grandchild. Was it male or female, he wondered?

October 10 Jacky Custis was still being offered advice. Washington has "given my full consent to the Sale of the Lands . . . [but] I should be wanting to myself, and guilty of an inexcusable act of remission and criminl. injustice to your Mother, not to secure an equivalent for her releasmt. of Dower." Washington despairs "of seeing my own home this Winter," he wrote brother John. For three years he had not been at Mount Vernon. The army settled in winter quarters from Danbury, Connecticut, to Middlebrook, New Jersey. Martha dreaded another trip to headquarters. "I am very uneasy at this time," she wrote her brother. "I have some reason to expect that I shall take another trip northward. . . . The poor General is not likely to see us here from what I can hear." Once again she would need to "summon her whole fortitude."

George met Martha in Philadelphia, where Congress had invited him to discuss army problems. The couple enjoyed city society for a time. "Your mother is with me here and well," George wrote Jacky with satisfaction. Martha tried to buy a doll for her brother's daughter. "Give little Patty a kiss for me. I have sent her a pair of shoes—there was not a Doll to be got in the city of Philadelphia."

*I*n February the Washingtons moved to commodious headquarters in Sommerville, New Jersey, four miles from the army at Middlebrook. New blue and red, and brown and red uniforms arrived from the French. The troops were "better clad and more healthy than they had ever been." But Washington was discouraged and disgusted by the slow progress of the state assemblies. "I really am not, nor shall I, I believe, be again surprised at anything," he wrote Jacky.

War speculaors appalled him. "Alas! What is virtue come to? what a miserable change has four years produced in the temper and dispositions of the Sons of America! It really shocks me to think of it!"

One family member had let him down. Betty's and Fielding's son George Lewis was causing "concern and resentment." He was absent from his regiment again. His father wrote that George wanted to resign from the army because he had not been promoted.

But visitors from Virginia cheered headquarters, and were entertained at a gala ball given by General Henry Knox and Lucy. At a party at General Greene's quarters Washington and Mrs. Greene "danced upwards of 3 hrs. without once sitting down . . . we had a pretty little frisk," wrote the host with satisfaction.

Six Delaware Indian chiefs came to camp in May. Martha and Lucy Knox and Kitty Greene watched the troops review. Some of the mounted savages were "farly fine-looking, but most of them appeared worse than Falstaff's gang," Martha reported.

Washington feared for Charlestown, South Carolina, which was under British attack. He expected a vigorous summer campaign in the north. In June "the Enemy moved up the North River in force," George wrote John. Martha headed south when the general moved his army to the Hudson too, as the enemy's shipping was "a source of much mischief and great perplexity to us."

In August Washington wrote Jacky from West Point that "we have given the enemy another little Stroke. . . . Our affairs at present put on a very pleasing aspect, especially in Europe and the West Indies. . . . Peace depends upon our Allies equally with ourselves."

Sister Betty Lewis visited Mount Vernon in September and sent a loving and positive report to her brother. She was "happy to find Sister Washington So hearty, and looks so well. . . . Could I of found you there it would of Compleat'd my Happiness, O when will that Day come that we shall meet again."

Not soon. The alliance with France had produced little more than uniforms. By November there had been no word of the French fleet since it arrived at Georgia to fight the British, Washington complained to Jacky. "We begin to fear that some great convulsion in the earth has caused a chasm between this and that state that can not be passed." Washington "is in the most disagreeable state of suspense," but asks Jacky to "Remember me affectionately to your uncles Bassett and Dandridge."

Late in December Martha rejoined the dispirited army at winter quarters in Morristown. Although there had been sporadic fighting, the northern campaign had not materialized. And when the American/land and French/sea attack on British-held Savannah failed, French General D'Estaing sailed away from America.

"THE BITTERNESS IN MY SOUL"—1780

*T*he winter at Valley Forge is renowned for its harshness, but the 1779–80 winter at Morristown was even more biting. Howling blizzards left four to six feet of snow on the ground. It was "intensely cold," Washington wrote Jacky. The soldiers were hungry and naked . . . in "the greatest distress on acct. of the want of provision we have ever felt. My love to Nelly and the Children" (now numbering three girls).

Martha helped as best she could. Observers spoke of her "Kindness to the sick and wounded . . . her intercessions with the Chief for the pardon of offenders." "I learn from the Virginia officers that Mrs. Washington seeking for objects of affliction and poverty, that she may extend to the sufferers the hand of kindness and relief."

May brought warmer weather and hopeful news. The French were sending an army as well as a fleet. Seven thousand to ten thousand soldiers would arrive under a general named de Rochambeau. Washington wrote cousin Lund a somewhat self-satisfied letter. "You ask how I am to be rewarded for all of this? There is one reward that nothing can deprive me of, and that is, the consciousness of having done my duty with the strictest rectitude, and most scrupulous exactness, and the certain knowledge, that if we should, ultimately fail in the present contest, it is not owning to the want of exertion in me, or the application of every means that Congress and the United States of the States individually, have put into my hands."

By July 6 "the bitterness of my Soul" had reemerged, Washington wailed to brother-in-law Fielding Lewis. The army was "low in ebb . . . [had been] five or Six days together without Meat; than as many without bread . . . numbers of men with scarcely as much cloathing as would cover their nakedness and at least a fourth of the whole with not even the shadow of a blanket severe as the Winter has been." How had these things come to pass?—"want of System, not to say foresight" on the part of Congress.

George wrote John the same day. "I derive much pleasure from hearing from you." But he is "wearied to death by the multiplicity of public matters." It has "ever been our conduct and misfortune to Slumber and Sleep while we should be diligent in preparation . . . affectionate regards to my Sister and all the family."

Martha had left or George's spirits might have been better. "The poor Genl . . . was so unhappy that it distressed me exceedingly," Martha wrote her brother-in-law.

"The Enemy after leaving the Jerseys, made demonstrations toward our Posts in the Highlands (on the North River) George wrote John. "This occasioned my moving that way . . . waiting the arrival of the French-fleet, and our own Reinforcements."

In August George simultaneously worried over the war and fretted over brother Samuel's bad health. Your letter "gave me much concern," George wrote him. "I sincerely wish you a perfect restoration of health and the enjoyment of every blessing of life." Sam had just married one of his five successive wives. "My best regards attend my Sister (with whom I should be happy in a better acquaintance.)" A French squadron was blocked at Newport, Rhode Island. "The flattering prospect which seemed to be opening to our view in the Month of May is vanishing like the Morning Dew."

Attempts to defeat the British in the states south of Virginia were largely unsuccessful. Benedict Arnold's treachery in September was "a scene of treason as shocking as it was unexpected." In December Martha returned to a demoralized husband. Headquarters this winter was near New Windsor on the Hudson.

"The Highest Pleasure and Satisfaction"—1781

*M*artha suffered with George as sickening reports arrived in January of mutiny among long-suffering Pennsylvania and New Jersey troops. Less important but irritating was the need for a good family steward. Martha pitched in as secretary, copying at least one of Washington's official letters.

In the Carolinas there was intense fighting. And in the Washingtons' own Virginia the British army plundered and burned under traitor Arnold. Washington sent General Lafayette and troops to the rescue. Governor Thomas Jefferson and the Virginia Assembly had to flee from the rampaging British. George and Martha knew that Mount Vernon was not immune to attack.

Devoted Washington biographers find it hard to forgive two of his family members for their behavior during these tense and discouraging times. Jacky Custis plagued him with money matters. "You might as well attempt to pay me in Old News Papers and Almanacks with which I can purchase nothing, as to give me paper money that has not a relative value to the Rent agreed on," Washington had thundered to Jacky in January, 1780. A year later came rumors that young Virginia Senator Custis had boycotted Assembly sessions when he didn't like the way they were going. From army headquarters his stepfather chastised him. "Be punctual in your attendance . . . hear dispassionately, and determine cooly all great questions . . . counteract . . . by steady and uniform opposition."

But Jacky the young husband of a young wife and father of four* tiny children, was understandably immersed in his own learning and responsibilities as a landholder and head of family. "I have been ever since I settled here [Abingdon] struggling with every Inconvenience that a Person can meet with in coming to a Plantation in every respect out of order." He probably boycotted the legislature because he thought it was an effective thing to do.

Washington's mother was an unrelenting financial burden. Late in 1778 she had complained to Lund: "I should Much obliged to you to send me forty pound Cash to by Corn for they have not Maid more at the Little Falls quarter then will Serve the plantation thear is terrible doing theare Charles never goes over I shall be Ruined Corn at five pound a barrel as for flower I dont know the taste of it I Never Lived soe pore in my Life butt if I Can gitt Corn, I am contented . . . I hear por Mrs. Washington is gon of [to join George] God bless you Spar your health or pore George will be Ruined."

Seventy-year-old Mary Ball Washington had not been feeling well when she complained to Lund of her situation. "The old lady has been very ill," her son-in-law Fielding Lewis wrote Washington the next month. She "is not out of danger and will soon be able to leave her room." From her point of view the commander in chief may have been thoughtless and irresponsible. He never wrote and had not been to see her in years.

*George Washington Parke Custis was born in 1781. He was "quite hearty," said his mother—"the prettiest creature in the world."

In March, 1781 came a humiliating letter from Benjamin
Harrison, Speaker of the Virginia house. As tactfully as he
could, Harrison explained that a move was under way to
provide a pension for Washington's mother. Martha was
visiting the Schuylers in Albany and could not hear Washington's anguished reply: "Before I left Virginia, I answered
all her calls for money; and since that period, have directed
my Steward to do the same. Whence her distresses can arise
therefore, I know not, never having received any complaint of his inattention or neglect. . . . Confident I am that
she has not a child that would not divide the last sixpence
to relieve her from *real* distress. This she has been repeat-
edly assured of by me; and all of us, I am certain would
feel much hurt, at having our mother a pensioner while we
had the means of supporting her . . . but in fact she has an
ample income of her own."

  Much is made by biographers of the number of times
Washington gave his mother money. He himself once made
the point in his diary that funds were given in the presence
of a brother. He would have a witness this time! But independent Mary was surely frustrated at being dependent on
handouts. Her frustation is mirrored in her son's frustration at having his army dependent on handouts begrudg-
ingly given by Congress.

  Harder to forgive is Mrs. Washington's lack of awareness
of the pressures her son was under and her stinginess with
praise. It is given as reluctantly as is his to younger members of the family. Mary's affection comes through, however. See her March 13, 1782 letter in the next section.

  When Martha returned to New Windsor from her visit
to the Schuylers, she may have comforted George with
thoughts of home. From still wintry New York a touching
letter went to Lund, aching with longing for Mount Vernon.

> How many Lambs have you had this Spring?
> How many Colts are you like to have?
> Is your covered ways done?
> What are you going about next?

Mrs. Washington had "taken a fancy to a Horse" Lund was to try and buy. "She joins me in best wishes for you Mrs. Washington and Milly Posey."

The next letter to Lund is heart-rending. The enemy had come to Mount Vernon. Although seventeen frightened slaves were stolen, the mansion was not burned. Loyal Lund had seen to that. But his reward was a cold blast from the north. "I am very sorry to hear of your loss; I am a little sorry to hear of my own, but that which gives me most concern, is, that you should go on board the enemys Vessels, and furnish them with refreshments. It would have been a less painful circumstance to me, to have heard, that in consequence of your non-compliance with their request, they had burnt my House, and laid the Plantation in ruins. You ought to have considered yourself as my representative, and should have reflected on the bad example of communicating with the enemy, and making a voluntary offer of refreshments to them with a view to prevent a conflagration."

Washington could not stay angry with Lund for long: "I am thoroughly perswaded that you acted from your best judgment. . . . Mrs. Washington joins me in best and affectionate regard for you."

A diary entry further reveals Washington's state of mind that spring: "Instead of having Magazines filled with provisions, we have a scanty pittance scattered here and there in the different States. Instead of having our Arsenals well supplied with Military Stores, they are poorly provided, and the Workmen all leaving them . . . and all that business [transportation] or a great part of it, being done by Military Impress, we are daily and hourly oppressing the people— souring their tempers—and alienating their affections."

A month later Martha's illness was another worry. "Mrs. Washington has been sick for more than ten days, and still continues so," Washington wrote Lund. She is "still weak and low . . . very desirous of seeing you," he told Jacky. Although Martha was not in danger, "I should be glad . . . if you could make her a visit."

The commander in chief had just returned from the important meeting with de Rochambeau at Wethersfield, Connecticut, that would lead to Yorktown. It had been agreed that the French troops in Rhode Island would join Washington's American ones in New York. Late in June Martha "set out . . . for Virginia—but with an intention to Halt at Philadelphia if from information and circumstances it was not likely she should remain quietly at Mount Vernon." His wife had left "in a very low and weak state," Washington wrote Fielding Lewis. "Remember me in the most Affectionate manner to my Sister."

Before heading south himself on the campaign that would end in victory, George penned a quick note to brother John. "Our Affairs during the whole Winter and spring, laboured under such complicated embarrassments and distress, that I had no time to write." To Sam he had confided earlier, "It is impossible for any person at a distance to have an idea of my embarrassments, or to conceive how an army can be kept together under any such circumstances as our is."

After a six-year absence it would have been impossible for George Washington to bypass Mount Vernon as he headed toward the British army to the south. He lingered there from September 9–11, inviting de Rochambeau and French officer Chastellux to join him—"to ease their Fatigue & to give them fresh Spirits to pursue our march the next Day." The sight of his beloved plantation and of Nelly and Jacky's four little children gave him fresh spirits. Stirred by the huge rejuvenated army, Jacky begged to join his stepfather. As usual, Washington gave in. October 12 Jacky wrote his mother from York: "The General tho in constant Fatigue looks very well." Jacky has stopped to see his Dandridge relatives on the way. Martha's stepmother wishes she would bring Bet and Pat to see her. The sight of Negroes stolen or encouraged to leave by the British shocks him. "The mortality that has taken place among the wretches is really incredible. I have seen numbers lying dead in the Woods and many so exhausted they cannot walk."

A week later General Washington sent a formal but joyous message to the president of Congress. October 19, 1781, from headquarters near York: "I have the Honor to inform Congress, that a Reduction of the British Army under the Command of Lord Cornwallis, is most happily effected. [The victory] has filled my Mind with the highest pleasure and Satisfaction."

The pleasure and satisfaction were tragically short-lived. Two weeks later twenty-eight-year-old Jacky Custis was dead of camp fever. A short stiff letter went to Congress from the Bassetts' ". . . an event which I met with at this place (very distressing to Mrs. Washington) will retard my arrival at Philadelphia a few days longer than I expected." From Mount Vernon a fuller explanation went to Lafayette. "I arrived at Eltham . . . [in] time enough to see poor Mr. Custis breathe his last; this unexpected and affecting event threw Mrs. Washington and Mrs. Custis (who were both present) into such deep distress. . . ."

Friends and strangers grieved for the family that had already sacrificed so much of itself for the country. November 19, 1781, Philadelphia, George Washington to Alexandria's citizens: "Your condolence for the loss of that amiable youth Mr. Custis, affects me most tenderly."

December 15, 1781, Philadelphia, George Washington to General Greene: "Poor Mrs. Washington . . . has met with a most severe stroke in the loss of her amiable Son, and only Child Mr. Custis."

December 25, 1781, Philadelphia, George Washington to Lord Stirling: "Mrs. Washington is better than I could have expected after the Heavy loss she met with."

George Washington expressed "no personal grief"[15] over Jack's death, says a biographer, implying a lack of love for the step-son. But he also expressed little grief years later when writing one of her sons about his sister Betty's death. The imperfection may be in George, not Jacky. More likely it is in us; we see an incomplete record.

15. Flexner, *George Washington* II, p. 471.

"LITTLE PROSPECT OF THE WAR'S ENDING"—1782

$\mathcal{G}$eorge's mother wrote him an affectionate letter in March which probably stirred up mixed emotions: "I was truly uneasy by not being at hom when you went thru fredireceksburg it was a onlucky thing for me now I am afraid I never Shall have that pleasure agin I am soe very unwell this trip over the Mountins has almost kill'd me I gett the 2 five ginnes you was soe kind to send me I am greatly obliged to you for it i was greatly shocht [missing—"at Jacky Custis's death"?]. . . pray give my kind love to Mrs. Washington and am My Dear Georg your Loveing and affectinat Mother."

To the general's mourning household at Newburg, New York, came the sad word of two more deaths in the family. "My Pore Dear Mr. Lewis," wrote sister Betty, "and my brother Sam both lay ill at the same time and it was the Lords will to take them to Himself, in three weeks one after the other." Fielding Lewis had worn himself out and impoverished his estate as chief commissioner for the manufacture of small arms for the army. "I have heard, and sincerely lament, the death of yr. Father," Washington wrote John Lewis, Fielding's son by his first wife. "My best love to my Sister and the family."

Of concern also was the matter of the legal care of Jacky and Nelly's four children. "If it is necessary to have a Guardian appointed to the Children . . . It is much my wish that you . . . should undertake this," Washington had begged Martha's brother Bartholomew Dandridge, the closest male, blood relative on their father's side. Uncle Dandridge hoped Washington could be their guardian, he replied. In the meantime they were "under the care of a very affectionate and prudent mother." (Nelly was twenty-three.) "I see very little prospect of the Wars ending," Washington wrote back. "It would be injurious to the Children, and madness in me" to take it on. "Such aid however, as it ever may be with me to give to the Children, especially the boy, I will afford with all my heart, and with all my Soul."

In June the matter still had not been settled. "I perceive your unwillingness to undertake the Guardianship," Washington wrote again, "It gives me much pleasure to hear that you, family and friends are well." But he wished Uncle Dandridge would see his duty.

Martha went home in July, returning to winter headquarters at Newburgh, New York, late in November. In France peace was being discussed. "We remain in the same state of uncertainty with respect to peace," Washington had written nephew George Augustine in September. "The prospects of the Campaign are perfectly inactive." In November he wrote again. "The Negociations are going on, but very limpingly." They must wait for Parliament to meet, he told brother-in-law Bartholomew Dandridge, "when the Parties for and against the American War will try their strength . . . we shall then know whether we are to settle down under our Vines and fig Trees in Peace, or prosecute the War."

"Glorious News of a General Peace"—
1783

*W*hile the commander in chief was cooling his heels, he sent for Isaac Watts's psalms and hymns for Martha, and wrote Lund for "two small (fore) teeth which I beg of you to wrap up carefully. . . ." He and Mrs. Washington were "sorry to hear that Mrs. [Lund] Washington has been delivered of a dead child, but very glad to find she is so well after it."

There was time for a letter of advice to brother John's twenty-one-year-old son Bushrod, the first of many avuncular letters he would write nephews in the years ahead. Bushrod was going to Philadelphia to study law. January 15, 1783, George Washington to Bushrod Washington: "I am not such a Stoic as to suppose you will . . . or ought . . . always to be in Company with Senators & Philosophers; but, of the young and juvenile kind let me advise you to be choice. It is easy to make acquaintances, but very difficult to shake them off [if] irksome and unprofitable. . . . Be cour-

teous to all, but intimate with few. . . . Let your *heart* feel
for the affliction, and distresses of every one, and let your
hand give in proportion to your purse. . . . Do not conceive
that fine Clothes make fine Men, any more than fine feathers make fine Birds. . . ."

Bushrod, in turn, was concerned over his sister Milly's
education back in Virginia. She should learn music and
French, he wrote his mother. If tutors were not to be had,
he would teach her himself when he got home. "A woman
should learn more than domestic duties." Bushrod also
wrote his mother a self-conscious, appealing letter about
the portrait of himself he had sent her. Friends had said
"the countenance is not an ill natured one, nor entirely
thoughtful, but rather a mixture of thought with Pensive-
ness. . . . I shall be anxious to hear your opinion," Bushrod
said.

The long wait for peace did nothing to help his uncle's
disposition. Brother Sam had died, leaving several young
children by his five wives. "[Your letter] gave me extreme
pain," George wrote John. "In Gods name how did my
Brothr. Saml. contrive to get himself so enormously in
debt?"

A letter from their mother "complains much *of the Knav-
ery of the Overseer at the little Falls Quarter*. . . . It is too much
while I am suffering in every other way (and hardly able to
keep my own Estate from Sale) to be saddled with all the
expence of hers." Could John tend to the matter? "I know
of none in whose hands it can be better placed," Washington said tactfully, "to none to whom it can be less inconvenient," he added sourly. The Benjamin Harrison letter "has
given and still continues to give me pain." Their mother
was "upon all occasions, and in all Companies complaining
of the hardness of the times, of wants and distresses; and
if not in direct terms, at least by innuendos inviting favors."
Her wants were imaginery. Would John "represent to her
in delicate terms the impropriety of her complaints and
acceptance of favors even when they are voluntarily offered,
from any but relations. It will not to do to touch upon this

subject in a letter to her, and therefore I have avoided it.
. . . With respect to Peace, we are held in a very disagreeable state of suspence," Washington concluded. He was
"sorry to find that my Sister was in bad health" and sent
"my love."

By March 19 there was still no word from the negotiators
abroad. There had been "a most insidious attempt to dis-
turb the repose of the army, and sow the seeds of discord
between the civil and military powers," Washington wrote
Lund. The "good sense, the virtue and patient forbearance
of the army . . . has again triumphed."*

On March 30, 1783 the commander in chief's usual
reserve in writing official letters broke down. To the president of Congress he sent "my warmest Thanks for the
Communication, you have been pleased to make to me and
the Army, of the glorious News of a General Peace. I have
the most lively sensations of gratitude and pleasure . . .
Effusion of Joy . . . on this happiest of Events."

During the wait for the British actually to leave the country Washington grew irritable again. John had written that
he feared George was "suffering greatly in rents." In June
a letter from Washington blasted Lund for not going out
and collecting them. Because of Lund's "aversion to going
from home" the chance had been lost to collect from "Tenants gone into the Western country many years arrears of
rent due." Naturally, Washington dreaded "going home to
empty coffers." Although annoyed at Lund, he could not
bear to realize that Lund had taken no wages for his years
of service. June 11, 1783, George Washington to Lund
Washington: "I shall be more hurt, than at any thing else,
to think that an Estate, which I have drawn nothing from,
for eight years, and which always enabled me to make any
purchase I had in view, should not have been able for the
last five years, to pay the manager."

Washington rightly anticipated "expensive living" when
he returned home because of the curious visitors who would

---

*The "Newburgh Address" by an anonymous writer urged the army to
hang on to its arms until Congress had given what it demanded.

swarm to Mount Vernon uninvited and in hospitable southern fashion be welcomed, if they had a letter of introduction. The needs of Sam's children, as well as Jacky's, preyed on his mind. There would be no berth in the navy for "our Nephew Ferdinand," he wrote John, because there would probably be no navy. Couldn't relatives on his mother's side help him find a place on a merchant ship? The taking on of their mother's affairs by John was appreciated. (No wonder George loved this particular brother.) He waited for "the Definitive Treaty . . . with much impatience." The American government under the shaky Articles of Confederation worried him. "We are a young Nation and have a character to establish."

In August Martha moved with George to Rocky Hill near Princeton. Congress was meeting there because unpaid, rioting soldiers made Philadelphia uncomfortable. In November word came at last that the peace treaty had been signed. The British evacuated New York. Martha and six wagonloads of papers and furnishings headed for Mount Vernon. Washington gave his "Farewell Orders to the Armies of the United States" and an emotional farewell to his officers at Fraunces's Tavern in New York. He journeyed to Congress, which was meeting this time at Annapolis, to resign his commission. After a moving ceremony and a gala ball, he went home on Christmas Eve to Mount Vernon where Martha was waiting for him.

He had not forgotten the grandchildren. In his saddlebags were: a locket, children's books, whirligig, and fiddle.

III

THE YEARS BETWEEN

1783–1789

"THE LITTLE FOLKS AND MRS. WASHINGTON"

*N*o person who had not the advantage of being present when General Washington received the intelligence of the peace, and who did not accompany him to his domestic retirement can describe the relief which that joyful event brought to his laboring mind, or the satisfaction with which he withdrew to the shades of private life,"[16] wrote an aide.

There was satisfaction in restoring his farms, which had suffered during his long absence. George refreshed his war-weary mind with thoughts of crop rotation, manure, the breeding of cattle, sheep and mules, his mill and fisheries. Daily he made the twenty-mile round of his farms. A 1786 census shows that 216 slaves worked on the entire estate; 67 of those were at the Mansion House Farm (41 grown people, 26 children).

16. Flexner, *George Washington* III (Boston, 1969), p. 6.

Martha Washington undoubtedly shared her husband's relief at being home. They were both in their fifties—tired and prone to sickness. At one point George was so troubled with rheumatism he carried his arm in a sling. Letters often referred to his wife's poor health. "Mrs. Washington enjoys but indifferent health. . . . [She is] too often troubled with bilious and cholicky complaints. . . . Mrs. W. .n is scarce ever well." And at last—"Mrs. Washington much less troubled with the bilious cholick."

During the years between the Revolution and the presidency Martha is a somewhat obscure figure. "Rather fleshy," wrote one stranger who came to Mount Vernon, "of good complexion, has a large portly double chin and an open and engaging Countenance, on which a pleasing smile sets during conversation, in which she bears an agreeable part." "Small and fat," wrote another. And a third—"hearty, comely, discreet, affable."

Martha's ladylike good taste is perceived in orders for personal articles. "Mrs. Wn [wants] fine thin handkerchiefs with striped or worked borders . . . articles . . . perfect in their kind." . . . Mrs. Washington understands that there is "very fine and pretty Dimmity Muslin selling on board the Indian Ship" and wishes some. Her graciousness and thoughtfulness are evident. She sent "particular thanks" to one of George's correspondents for flower roots and seeds and "will preserve in the manner directed." She visited the sick of all ages. To Mme. Lafayette she sent a barrel of Virginia hams. "You know the Virginia Ladies value themselves on the goodness of their bacon," George Washington wrote Lafayette. "We recollect that it is a dish of which you are fond."

Into her ample bosom Martha affectionately gathered stray nieces and grandchildren. Deceased sister Nancy Bassett's daughter Fanny came to stay. "She is a child to me, and I am very lonesome when she is absent," wrote her aunt when Fanny was on a visit. Martha's stepmother and her remaining brother, Bartholomew Dandridge, died the same day; Bartholomew's daughter Patty was made welcome at Mount Vernon. Harriot Washington, Sam's orphaned daughter, moved in when she was nine.

Daughter-in-law Eleanor (Nelly) Custis was a "charming, likeable young widow [with a] gay and prepossessing nature," according to one smitten observer. No longer in mourning, Nelly went to balls but did not enjoy them—"the description of one wou'd serve for twenty, except the differences in partners, and their the only variety is the name for they mostly have the same, I Love and I Despair, Countenances I wonder the mortals are not tired of acting the same farce over so often, when the audience shew so few signs of approbation." She had not married again, Nelly assured Kitty Greene. ". . . no such thought has ever enter'd My Head as yet nor do I believe ever will."

But to Washington's surprise (and apparently, to Nelly's) thirty-year-old Dr. David Stuart of Alexandria wooed and won her. "Mrs. Custis has never suggested in any of her Letters to Mrs. Washington . . . the most distant attachment to D.S.," Washington wrote cousin Lund. "But if this should be the case, and she wants advice upon it, a Father and Mother are . . . most proper to be consulted. I never did, nor do I believe ever shall give advice to a woman who is setting out on a matrimonial voyage."

Eleanor Custis's older children Betsey and Patty remained at Abingdon with their mother and her new husband, but made frequent visits to Mount Vernon. Five-year-old Nelly and three-year-old George Washington Parke Custis (called "Tub" or "Wash" or "Boy" by his grandmother) went to live permanently with the Washingtons, but made frequent visits to Abingdon. Nelly had already spent much of her life at Mount Vernon. At birth her mother was ill, so she was taken there to a wet nurse and cared for by Lund Washington's childless wife.

"The little folks enjoy perfect health," their step-grandfather wrote a friend with satisfaction a year after his return to Mount Vernon. Washington wanted a tutor for the children who would also help answer his voluminous mail, and sent letters on the subject to friends and acquaintances

on both sides of the Atlantic. Tutoring "will be very trifling
'til the Children are a little more advanced." They were
both "very promising," but "of an age when close confinement may be improper." Washington meant "to fit the boy
... for a University." It was essential that he be taught
French grammatically since French was "now becoming a
part of the education of youth in this Country." The sec-
retary-tutor "will sit at my Table, will live as I live, will mix
with the Company . . . be treated . . . with civility." It was
important that he have proper diction and a good hand,
since the children would copy it.

In the early summer of 1786 Tobias Lear of New Hampshire answered the call. "Mr. Lear arrived here a few days
ago," Washington wrote his sponsor, General Benjamin
Lincoln, "and appears to be a genteel, well-behaved young
man." The tutor had his hands full. Wash was "as fat and
saucy as ever . . . as full of spirits as an eggshell is of meat
. . . the same clever boy you left him," according to his loving grandparents. His outgoing nature charmed guests.
"Your young friend is in high health," Washington wrote a
recent visitor. He says, "I beg [you] will make hast and come
here again." With Lear's help six-year-old Wash composed
an affectionate letter to a former tutor Gideon Snow.

"Dear Snow: I should be very happy to see you here if
you can find time to come down. When will you send my
waggon to me? For my old one is almost worn out and I
shall have none to get in my harvest with."

After he had been there almost two years Lear wrote to
a close friend at home.

"For the first 4 or 5 months after I came here I thought
I observed in the General a greater degree of reserve and
coldness toward me than he shewed to any other person
. . . a different conduct towards me led me to see that caution and circumspection (striking traits in his Character)
had induced this behavior; for, from that period, he began
to relax and gradually drew me towards him by every tender
and endearing tie. . . . I am treated in every respect as a
child of it [this family], and at the same time feel happy in

having placed myself in this point of view without sacrific-
ing a single spark of that independence of mind which
ought to govern every man who is worthy to live. Mrs.
Washington is everything that is benevolent and good—I
honor her as a second mother.

"A little Grandson of Mrs. Washington's and his Sister,
the one of 6 and the other of 8 years old afford me no small
pleasure and amusement in instructing them, they are,
without partiality, as fine children as ever were seen, I never
thought I could be so much attached to children as I am to
them.

"George Washington is, I believe, almost the only man
of an exalted character who does not lose some part of his
respectability by an intimate acquaintance.[17]"

It was a period of relative tranquility for Washington.
Farm life was demanding but satisfying. As before the war,
his interests were regional. Washington resumed his attention to a prewar plan for draining Virginia's Great Dismal
Swamp in order to harvest timber. He responded enthusi-
astically to rejuvenated efforts to create a trade route by
road and canal between the Ohio River and Tidewater.

Domestic life was comfortable with a companionable and
undemanding wife and four appealing grandchildren.
Betsey, Patty, and Nelly Custis are mentioned in their step-
grandfather's writings briefly but fondly. "All well except
Miss Custis, who still feels the effect, and sometimes the
return of her fever. . . . Patcy has been a little unwell but
better. . . . Betsy Custis home with me."

Martha ordered a collar for her granddaughters from
Mrs. Powel, a Philadelphia friend, which by means of a
screw device would hold up their heads and force them to
throw back their shoulders. A ribbon concealed the screw.
"The girls will wear them with pleasure," their grandmother said firmly. Mrs. Powel sent "our little favorite"
Wash, a book. "Boy is so pleased with the book you sent
him . . . has read it over and over," Martha wrote. Wash

17. Original letter owned by Massachusetts Historical Society.

was "the pet of the family," his grandmother's "pretty little Dear Boy."

At the war's end an aide of Baron von Steuben wrote admiringly of Martha Washington. "She reminded me of the Roman matrons of whom I had read so much, and I thought that she well deserved to be the companion and friend of the greatest man of the age." She remained both friend and companion, dependable and sturdy. In letter after letter especially to the Powels, the Knoxes, the Greenes, the Robert Morrises, and other friends from the wartime years, Washington included a warm message from his wife. "Mrs. Washington sends her compliments . . . joins me in affectionate regards . . . unites in best wishes for yourself." Martha frequents the diaries: "with Mrs. W. to mill and new barn . . . set out for F[redericksburg] acc. by Mrs. W. on a visit to my mother. . . . Alex. with Mrs. W. wanted to get some cloathing for little Washington Custis."

In 1784 and 1785 sculptors came to Mount Vernon to make plaster casts of Washington's face. Martha's reaction to the unexpected sight of her husband stretched out on his back with plaster on his face amused George. She "involuntarily exclaimed. . . . Her cry excited in me a disposition to smile, which gave my mouth a slight twist."

Affection for the army was a continuing bond. "It's astonishing with what raptures Mrs. Washington spoke about the discipline of the army," observed a visitor, ". . . the excellent order they were in, superior to any troops, she said, upon the face of the earth, towards the close of the war. Even the English acknowledge it, she said. What pleasure she took in the sound of the fifes and drums, preferring it to any music that has ever heard! And then to see them reviewed a week or two before they were disbanded, when they were all well clothed, was, she said a most heavenly sight." Letters home during the Constitutional Convention that took Washington to Philadelphia in 1787 show Martha's and George's mutual interest in the plantation— in decorated moldings for the new room, a cupola with bird and olive branch, buckles and knives, a new coach dog ("for the . . . benefit of Madame Moose; her amorous fits should therefore be attended to," wrote President of the Convention Washington.)

But there were large areas not shared. While her husband followed with intense concern Shay's rebellion in Massachusetts and calls for a convention to revise the Articles of Confederation, Martha tended to her hams and preserves. As the new Constitution made its passage through state legislatures during 1787 and '88, Martha wrote her niece Fanny, "We have not a simple article of news but pollitick which I do not concern myself about." Perhaps she wished to avoid thinking of the inevitable result of ratification. How did Martha react, one wonders, to English houseguest Catherine Macaulay Graham, author of the eight-volume *History of England,* ardent supporter of the American colonies' independence, interested observer of their attempt to govern themselves? George was impressed with Mrs. Graham and brought out his military records for her "perusal and amusement." He wrote later, "A Visit from a Lady so celebrated in the Literary world could not but be very flattering to me. . . . Her sentiments respecting the inadequacy of the powers of Congress . . . coincide with my own."

Was Martha impressed? Mrs. Graham "whose agreeable company we have had the pleasure of a few days" had been introduced by Bostonian Mercy Warren. But she wore rouge! She had taken as a second husband a man thirty-four years younger! The two women might as well have been of a different species for all they had in common. Yet "Mrs. Washington . . . has a grateful sense of your favorable mention of her," Washington penned politely in a reply to Mrs. Graham's bread and butter letter.

When his fellow Virginians had insisted that George participate in the 1787 convention in Philadelphia which produced the Constitution, Martha refused to accompany him. "Mrs. Washington is become too domestick, and too attentive to two little Grand Children to leave home," George wrote Robert Morris. He was reluctant to go himself. "I am quite homesick," he wrote from Philadelphia.

During the postwar years at Mount Vernon did George Washington secretly yearn for the power to lead his countrymen? Did he dream dreams of more exciting, less "domestick" women? "In my estimation," he wrote in 1785, "more permanent and genuine happiness is to be found in the sequestered walks of connubial life, than in the giddy rounds of promiscuous pleasure, or the more tumultous and imposing scenes of successful ambition."

"Your Friend and Uncle"

*W*ould Washington's happiness have been even more genuine and permanent had he children of his own? A remarkable letter written in 1786 to a nephew reveals that in George's opinion it was not because of himself that he was childless. "If Mrs. Washington should survive me there is moral certainty of my dying without issue, and should I be the longest liver, the matter in my opinion is almost as certain; for whilst I retain the reasoning faculties I shall never marry a girl and it is not probable that I should have children by a woman of an age suitable to my own should I be disposed to enter into a second marriage." Eighteenth-century manners and George Washington's restraint do not allow a glimmer of his feelings about the subject. What is apparent from his writings, however, is the affection and deep caring he poured into his relationships with his nephews.

George Augustine Washington, brother Charles's son, had not disappointed his uncle during the war. He commanded the life guards, fought at Princeton, served as an aide de camp at Valley Forge and to Lafayette at the end of the war. Poor health plagued the young man. As Lawrence Washington had years before, George Augustine tried to get well in Bermuda. "My nephew . . . has been buffeting the seas from clime to clime, in pursuit of health, but poor fellow! I believe in vain," wrote Washington. His nephew is "a very amiable young man for whom I have an entire affection and regard."

Young George spent the winter of 1785 in Charleston, South Carolina. His uncle was glad he had "left the Island of Bermuda with encreased health," but fretted over the journey from South Carolina to Mount Vernon. Washington suggested that George travel via packetboat to Philadelphia and by stage to Alexandria "to avoid the dreary roads and bad accomodation through North Carolina."

Fond as he was of his uncle, young George was drawn to Mount Vernon by Martha's niece Fanny Bassett. He arrived in May 1785, "much amended in health but not quite free from the disorder in his breast." George wants Fanny to marry him, Washington wrote his brother-in-law Burwell Bassett. "It has ever been a maxim with me thro' life, neither to promote, nor to prevent a matrimonial connection, unless there should be something indispensably requiring interference in the latter; I have always considered marriage as the most interesting event of one's life; the foundation of happiness or misery; to be instrumental therefore in bringing two people together who are indifferent to each other, and may soon become objects of hatred; or to prevent a union which is prompted by mutual esteem and affection, is what I never could reconcile to my feelings; and therefore, neither directly nor indirectly have I ever said a syllable to Fanny or George upon the subject of their intended connexion, but as their attachment to each other seems to have been early formed, warm and lasting, it bids fair to be happy: if therefore you have no objection, I think the sooner it is consummated the better."

October 15, 1785 Fanny and George became "one bone and one flesh," Washington wrote a correspondent with satisfaction. "After the candles were lighted George Auge. Washington and Frances Bassett were married by Mr. Grayson," he recorded in his diary.

Cousin Lund Washington, who had managed Washington's plantation so faithfully during the war, longed for retirement. "I shall always retain a grateful sense of your endeavors to serve me," Washington wrote him. "Nothing but the entire confidence which I reposed could have made me easy under an absence of almost nine years from my family and Estate." Because of Lund he had been able to give "not only my time but my whole attention to the public concerns of this Country."

Washington hoped that George Augustine would take Lund's place as manager of the plantation, but did not know "his plans or wishes." Fanny and George had been told they could "make this House their home 'till the squalling and trouble of children might become disagreeable," Washington wrote Lund. He had not repeated the offer, he said rather huffily, because an offer made once should be sufficient. But it "is hardly to be expected," he added with understanding, "that two people young as they are . . . would like confinement."

Perhaps Martha had a quiet talk with Fanny. A month later Washington wrote briskly that George and Fanny would make Mount Vernon "a permanent residence" and George will "attend to the business of the plantation."

The arrangement must have been satisfactory to Washington. At about the time of the young couple's first anniversary he wrote his nephew that he planed to leave him two thousand to three thousand acres of property. This was not "a hint for you to prepare another home . . . [but because of] the double ties by which you are connected with this family (to say nothing of the favourable opinion we entertain of you.)"

Lawyer Bushrod Washington, brother John Augustine's son, was another nephew Washington could count on to help loyally with his affairs. The first fall back at Mount Vernon Washington planned "a visit to my Lands on the

Western Waters" and to reconnoiter a trade route from the upper Potomac to the Ohio. Only his old friend and companion Dr. Craik, and his son William, would accompany him. But he "would take [Bushrod] with me with pleasure," Washington wrote his brother.

The next year while Bushrod was at Richmond (which had become Virginia's capital), his uncle called upon him for several errands. "As you are now at the fountain head of information," would Bushrod send a copy of the ordinances passed? Would he put an advertisement in the paper of the May meeting of the proprietors of the Great Dismal Swamp, and ask about his uncle's taxes on the western lands?

Advice was forthcoming—Washington had reservations about the "Patriotic Society" Bushrod had joined, a sort of citizens lobby. It might work against a national government, Washington feared. But he could be jocular with his nephew. The mule Washington had acquired from the king of Spain's stables was not performing. "If Royal gift will administer, he shall be at the Service of your Mares, but at present he seems too full of Royalty, to have anything to do with a plebean race; perhaps his Stomach may come to him, if not, I shall wish he had never come from his most Catholic Majesty's Stables."

And Washington could express his fondness for his nephew and family. "I had heard with much concern of your illness. Be careful in guarding against a relapse, by taking cold . . . offer me affectionately to all. . . . love to you and Nancy."

Bushrod's father, John, remained "My dear brother" for whom Washington would ask neighbor George Mason for a loan and be his security, seek jobs for his sons, and to whom he sent "every good wish . . . every sentiment of regard and affection." John sent George "a Swan, 4 wild Geese and two Barrels of Holly Berries," and brought his wife Hannah, daughter Milly, and sons for a visit at the time of the Alexandria races.

Washington suffered with John over "the untimely death

of my son Augustine which has affected me greatly. . . .
The shock was too great for her [Hannah's] infirm frame.
She fell into a convulsion." Poor John himself had the gout
and hobbled across the floor on crutches. He could still offer
to his brother a selfless "congratulates on your successes . . .
that you may long enjoy good health and every blessing
this world can afford is my most ardent wish."

January 10, 1787 a grieving Washington wrote in his
diary: "I rec'd by express the acct. of the sudden death (by
a fit of Gout in the head) of my beloved Brother, Colo. Jno.
Auge. Washington. At home all day." To nephew Bushrod
Washington wrote: "I condole most sincerely with you, my
Sister and family, on the death of my Brother. I feel most
sensibly for this event." To Lafayette (explaining the black
seal on his letter) he said simply, "I have lately lost a
Brother." And to Henry Knox, I have "just buried a
Brother who was the intimate companion of my youth, and
the friend of my ripened age."

Yet in that initial letter to Bushrod, Washington's often
expressed, deeply felt belief in acceptance of God's will
reveals itself—"resignation being our duty, to attempt an
expression of my sorrow on this occasion would be as fee-
bly described, as it would be unavailing when related."

Washington offered his services to the family, but could
not be executor of his brother's estate. "Your competency
alone is sufficient for this purpose (when joined by that of
my Sister and your brother)" he wrote Bushrod. "The task
will be easy . . . an alleviating circumstance of my brother's
death that his affairs fall into such good hands. . . . Every
good wish . . . sincerest regard . . . unfeined Affection."

At the end of the year Bushrod was back in Richmond
as a member of the Assembly considering the proposed
federal Constitution. His uncle, who ardently wanted passage, suggested techniques which had always served him
well—"speak seldom, but to important Subjects (except such
as particularly relate to your Constituents) . . . make yourself *perfect* master of the Subject. Never exceed a *decent*
warmth, and submit your sentiments with diffidence."

When Washington had left for Philadelphia in May of 1787 for the Convention which produced the Constitution, he left nephew George Augustine Washington in charge of Mount Vernon. (He and Fanny had just had their first child, which lived only a few days.) Do not get fatigued in doing my business, Washington cautioned his frail nephew. Be careful about staying out in the sun.

But there was "no prospect of a Speedy return (for contrary to my wish, I am made, by a unanimous vote President of the Convention)," he soon wrote from Philadelphia. Manure must be attended to . . . the mill race . . . ditching . . . brick making . . . plowing . . . wheat, barley, oats, corn . . . shrubberies . . . cills layed and honeysuckle nailed up. As in the letters to Lund during the war, no detail was too small to concern Mount Vernon's master. Had the mares been sent to the jacks? "If the Jacks do not perform what expected from them, the Mares unquestionably, must be sent to Magnolio." Drought was a severe problem. "I see no more than the Man in the Moon where I am to get money to pay my Taxes, etc., etc., etc., if I have made no crop, & shall have to buy Corn for my people."

The procedings of the Convention were secret and Washington kept them so. "The sentiment of the different members seem to accord more than I expected," was the only comment he allowed himself. In every letter he sent "Love to Fanny . . . best wishes to Mr. Lear . . . remember me affectionately to all at home." And once—"P.S. Have you thinned the Carrots which were too thick?"

Two years later when George Washington left Mount Vernon for New York and the first presidency, the letters to loyal George Augustine resumed. "It is neither my desire nor wish that you should become a drudge to my Affairs. . . . Ever your warm friend and Affectionate Uncle."

George Steptoe and Lawrence Washington, brother Sam's young orphaned sons, were a worry. Washington sent George Augustine to Berkeley County to see about a sale of Sam's Negroes to raise money for his boys. Brother

Charles, who lived nearby, was supposed to be in charge of Sam's estate. "Let your father [Charles] know, in explicit terms," Washington wrote George Augustine, "that if he will not keep me furnished with the means to defray the expences of these boys that he must take the whole of their affairs on himself." A year later nephew Bushrod was urged to go to Berkeley and examine Sam's affairs. "I have reason to believe, the hours of your Uncle Charles are spent in intoxication," Washington told Bushrod.

George Washington was responsible for his young nephew's education. In the fall of 1784 he had entered George Steptoe and Lawrence in the Reverend Stephen Balch's Academy at Georgetown, Maryland. He wanted them "taught the French language and such parts of the Mathematic's as will bring them acquainted with practical Surveying." As he had when Jacky Custis was in school thirteen years earlier, Washington believed surveying, "useful to every man who has landed property." Mr. Balch "speaks in favorable terms" of George Steptoe and would receive their mutual nephews into his own family, Washington assured Charles (who at this point was apparently sober) the next spring. Washington sent "most affectionate regards" to his brother.

"If it is your opinion they are doing well where they are, I think they had as well continue," Charles concurred. He enclosed some money. "I am Dr. Sir with great regard your Loving Brother."

Instructions concerning the nephews were fired off by George to all concerned. They were "desirous of going to the Dancing School in Georgetown" and had his permission. Washington wanted "their morals as well as education . . . attended to, and tho' I do not desire they should be deprived of necessary and proper amusements, yet it is my earnest request that they may be kept close to studies." Mr. Bailey, the Georgetown storekeeper with whom the nephews boarded, was not to indulge them "in any extravagance, or with anything improper." Nor should they be given pocketmoney "unless the necessity is apparent."

The Reverend Mr. Balch did not receive them into his own family after all. Washington had expected them to board with him, he chided Balch. "Mr. Bayly . . . declines boarding them after the 24th." Because of that and because of the expense of Georgetown, George Steptoe and Lawrence were to be "removed" and enrolled at the school in Alexandria. Charles was "sorry to hear the two little boys are at a place where they are gaining so little Improvement at so high an Expence." Their estate was in terrible shape, but he had "mustered up some money. . . . I labour under many afflictions on Acct. of the Orphans," Charles reminded George. "Your most affectionate brother."

Plantation demands, construction of the Potomac canal, Constitution writing and ratification could not deter George Washington from his avuncular duties. George Steptoe was greatly concerned over a letter from his uncle which criticized his learning, he wrote Washington. He did *not* allow "a thought of dress and pleasure" to interfere with his studies. He *was* "defective in the spelling and writeing of english . . . as I always paid more attention to my lattin." Uncle Washington had insinuated that George Steptoe's older half-brother Ferdinand was "the object of my immitation." George Steptoe was "sensible of [Ferdinand's] unbecoming conduct and altogether disapprove of it." There is no explanation of what Ferdinand's unbecoming conduct was. Washington made no comment when he noted in his diary the next year: "G.S. to Lancaster to visit Ferdinando W. who lay dangerously ill of a consumption."

At first Washington was satisfied with Alexandria merchant Samuel Hanson, with whom his nephews now boarded—"under the eye of a Gentleman as capable as you." But George Washington was no longer the inexperienced, somewhat awed guardian who corresponded before the war with Jacky's schoolmaster Jonathan Boucher. His March 18, 1788 letter to Hanson is shrewd. "Your candid and free communications respecting the conduct of my Nephews . . . deserve my best thanks, and I should think myself inexcusable, if, [not] equally open and candid" concerning allegations from them. They are sometimes late for school because breakfast is not early enough . . . sometimes go without any. They aren't invited to dine with company, are served indifferently in another place afterwards. Shirts are washed in lye without soap and destroyed. "This communication, Sir, cannot, I think, be displeasing to a person of your candor. I do not state the above as facts but merely as the reports of the boys, and if they should live with you again it will undoubtedly have a good effect by shewing them that their reports will always be made known to you, and the truth or falsehood of them discovered."

May 5 Washington sent George Steptoe a mild reproof: "Mr. Hanson informs me that you slept from home three nights successively, and once contrary to his express prohibition . . . complaints of this nature are extremely painful to me." To Mr. Hanson he expressed his gratitude that Lawrence, on the other hand, had behaved so well. He had "suspected that trespass would have commenced on his part."

By July Washington was fed up with his nephews' education. (A few days later news of New York's unconditional ratification of the Constitution sweetened his mood.) "Want of Arithmetical and Mathematics instructor at [the Alexandria] Academy is . . . a very great defect." His nephews couldn't write legibly. There were students at the academy who had spent six or seven years at the classics, but were "*entirely* unacquainted with these parts of literature to fit them for the *ordinary* purposes of life." Washington's nephews would be withdrawn unless there was a change.

August 6 there was trouble again. Lawrence was at Mount Vernon, Washington wrote Hansen, "afraid to remain at your house. When Lawrence had misbehaved, Hanson had beaten him. He had bruises to show for it. Washington was prepared to "correct" Lawrence for misbehaving. "But he begged so earnestly and promised so faithfully that there should be no cause of complaint against him for the future that I have suspended the Punishment." But Washington had a few words of chastisement for Hanson. His nephews

were of an "*age* and *size* now as to be a fitter subject to be
reasoned with than to receive corporal punishment." His
primary object in placing them with Hanson had been that
they be "treated more on the footing of Friendship, and as
companions, than as *mere* School-boys." To George Steptoe
who had tried to protect his brother, Washington wrote
sternly:

"It was with equal pain and surprise that I was informed
. . . of your unjustifiable behavior in rescuing your brother
from that chastisement, which was due to his improper
conduct." Washington wants "justice done," but there are
"proper modes." There should be "fair and candid repre-
sentation of facts . . . not . . . vague complaints, disobedi-
ence . . . which make enemies. . . . If the admonitions of
friendship are lost, other methods must be tried." Washington wants his nephews "to turn out well. . . . [I am] very
desirous of continuing your affectionate uncle."

The following February while Washington was expecting the dreaded call back to public life the boys were still in
Alexandria—and growing. "Your humble and dutifull
nephew" George Steptoe wrote for "a pair of breeches
apiece a hat a pair of shoes and buckles for me and a few
pocket handkerchiefs. . . . It is entirely by your goodness
that we are enabled to remaine in Town," he acknowledged.

Washington wrote him in March. "It is possible I shall
soon be under the necessity of quitting this place. . . . You
have now arrived to that age when you must quit the trifling amusements of a boy, and assume the more dignified
manners of a man." George Steptoe and Lawrence were to
board with their uncle's friend Dr. Craik and his estimable
wife. That would be "pleasing and profitable to you." There
were to be no complaints or "you may depend upon losing
that place which you now have in my affections. . . . But if
your conduct is such as to merit my regard, you may always
depend upon the warmest attachment, and sincere affection of Your friend and Uncle."

Sister Betty's fatherless children were never far from George's consciousness. Relations with his sister were cordial enough. "Planted filberts given me by my Sister Lewis . . . planted some Cobb nuts (given me by my sister L.) . . . lodged at Sister Lewis's (after visiting my mother) . . . dined with my sister Lewis in Fredericksburg." Relationships with Betty's numerous boys varied. In one instance it was downright hostile. To Fielding Lewis, Jr., Washington wrote: "Altho' your disrespectful conduct towards me, in coming into this country and spending weeks therein without ever coming near me, entitles you to very little notion or favor from me; yet I consent that you may get timber from off my Land . . . to build a house . . . in Recter town . . . now let me ask you what your views were in purchasing a Lott in a place which, I presume, originated with and will end in two or three Gin Shops. . . ."

Fielding was not in the least intimidated. "I am gratefully Obliged to you for the timber you was pleased to give me . . . and am sorry that it never has been in my power to come to see you since. . . . Oweing to the Distressed Situation I have been in . . . your mentioning my being in Fairfax and never going to see you is Very Right, but when there I was obliged to be every day indeavoring to make up money to discharge my debts—and should not have enjoyed my self in Seeing you when in Such a Situation— but now being Cleare of Debt I hope to Spend two or three weakes with you in Some Satisfaction—." The letter was delivered by Fielding's young son, about whom he had the nerve to declare: "Perhaps you may want him in some business or other, should it be the Case he may continue with you till of Age Should you not want him you will oblige me in getting him into busniss."

Five years later Fielding was again in debt. Betty wrote her brother, "Fielding is so distrest that his Children would go naked if it was not for the assistance I give him."

Washington preferred to initiate offers to nephews in need. As job applications poured in even before he had been formally elected president, George wrote Betty that he would be willing to employ her son Bob as a secretary. Bob should reply immediately "as there are hundreds who would be glad to come in." Betty must have communicated to her son the need for speedy action. Bob had accepted the offer by the time his uncle wrote again a little over a week later. Washington was to ride to New York before his wife. (Tobias Lear had left already.) When Washington's horses had gotten back to Mount Vernon, Martha and the children would follow and Bob should accompany them.

April 16, 1789 Washington wrote in his diary: "I bade adieu to Mount Vernon, to private life, and to domestic felicity, and with a mind oppressed with more anxious and painful sensations than I have words to express, set out for New York."

"My Mother"

Meanwhile, what of Mary, the mother of Washington? The weather had kept him from seeing her the winter of 1784, he wrote a correspondent. "I shall soon be enabled, I expect, to discharge that duty on which Nature and inclination have a call," he added piously. In 1785 "spent half an hour with my Mother," Washington wrote in his diary.

Two years later a flowery letter to Lafayette's wife said, "My Mother will recieve the compliments you honor her with as a flattering mark of your attention; and I shall have great pleasure in delivering them myself." One questions how soon Washington galloped to Fredericksburg with the compliments, and when he did if Mary was any more impressed than she had been by her son's acquaintance with other illustrious folk.

"I am quite glad to hear you and all the family is well," Mary wrote faithful John Washington one day when she was feeling low. "I am going fast, and it, the time, is hard. . . . I never lived soe poore in my life. Was it not for Mr. French and your sister Lewis I should be almost starved, but I am like an old almanack quite out of date. Give my love to Mrs. Washington [and] all the family. I am dear Johnne your loving and affectionate Mother."

As outsiders often do, a neighbor saw a less self-pitying, more admirable woman. "She goes about the neighborhood, to visit our quality on foot, with a cane in her hand, and sometimes—a Negro girl walking behind her, to assist her in case of necessity. . . . She must be near 80 years old . . . and talks of *George* without the least pride or vanity . . . she will not keep any Carriage, but a Chaise and two old family horses. . . . She lives in a little house of one story . . . windows are always shut and barred . . . for she delights to live in a little back room or two, where I have seen her sitting at work, with a slave to attend her—such is her taste."

When John died in 1787, Washington may have truly believed that "resignation" to the will of God was his "duty." But it did not keep him from unloading his unhappiness on his mother. He wrote her a lengthy, blistering letter, which exploded decades of resentment and anger at her attempts to make him feel guilty. George Augustine had sent word that she wanted money, so with the letter her son was reluctantly sending her fifteen guineas ". . . which believe me is all I have, and which indeed ought to have been paid many days ago to another." It is "hard upon me when you have taken everything you wanted from the Plantation by which money could be raised." George has recieved nothing from it himself for more than twelve years, if ever. He has paid his mother on the other hand, £260 by Lund's figuring and £50 out of his own pocket plus what was raised by crops.

"I sincerely lament [the death] of my brother John . . . on many accounts, and on this painful event condole with you most sincerely. I do not mean . . . to withhold any aid or support . . . whilst I have a shilling left, you shall have a part . . . but I want credit [not to be] viewed as a delinquent, and considered perhaps by the world as [an] unjust and undutiful son."

Washington advised his mother to rent land and Negroes to Bushrod. It would "ease you of all care and trouble . . . make your income certain." She should "break up house-keeping, hire out all the rest of your servants but a man and a maid, and live with one of your children. This would relieve you entirely from the cares of this world, and leave your mind at ease to reflect undisturbably on that which ought to come." John had agreed and had wanted her with him. But John was gone. "My house is at your service, and [I] would press you most sincerely and most devoutly to accept it, but I am sure, and candor requires me to say, it will never answer your purposes in any shape whatsoever. For in truth it may be compared to a well resorted tavern" filled with strangers. You would be obliged "to do one of 3 things: 1st, to be always dressing to appear in company; 2d, to come into [the room] in a dishabille, or 3d, to be as it were a prisoner in your own chamber. The first you'd not like; indeed, for a person at your time of life it would be too fatiguing. The 2d, I should not like, because those who resort here are, as I observed before, strangers and people of the first distinction. And the 3d, more than probably, would not be pleasing to either of us . . . calmness and serenity of mind, which in my opinion you ought now to prefer to every other consideration in life. . . . A man, a maid, the phaeton and two horses, are all you should want.

"There are such powerful reasons in my mind for giving this advice that I cannot help urging it with a degree of earnestness which is uncommon for me to do. . . . It is, I am convinced the only means by which you can be happy . . . for happiness depends more upon the internal frame of a person's own mind, than on the externals in the world. Of the last, if you will pursue the plan here recommended, I am sure you can want nothing that is essential. The other depends wholly upon yourself, for the riches of the Indies cannot purchase it.

"Mrs. Washington, George and Fanny join me in every

good wish for you, and I am, honored madame, your most dutiful and aff. son."

There is no record of Mary's verbal reaction to the letter. Two months later as Washington was about to leave for the Constitutional Convention in spite of painful rheumatism, he was summoned by an express to Fredericksburg "not a moment to be lost to see a mother and *only* sister (who are supposed to be in the agonies of Death) expire." Washington hastened "to obey this melancholy call." He found his mother "reduced . . . to a Skeleton." His "affectionate Sister['s] . . . watchful attention to my Mother during her illness had brought [Betty] to death's door." But fortunately, both mother and sister were now out of danger. So Washington hurried along to Philadelphia.

Perhaps the letter helped Washington's relationship with his mother. At least George had given her his full attention for a change. The following year he spoke more kindly of his "aged and infirm parent." In July, 1789 the president received a letter from Betty. "My mother's [cancerous] Breast still continues bad. [She is] sensible of it and is Perfectly resign'd—wishes for nothing more than to keep it easy. She wishes to hear from you; she will not believe you are well till she has it from under your hand."

September 1 Mary Washington died. "My dear Sister," George wrote Betty: "Awful, and affecting as the death of a Parent is, there is consolation in knowing, that Heaven has spared ours to an age, beyond which few attain, and favored her with the full enjoyment of her mental faculties, and as much bodily strength as usually falls to the lot of fourscore. Under these considerations and a hope that she is translated to a happier place, it is the duty of her relatives to yield due submission to the decrees of the Creator. When I was last at Fredericksburg, I took a final leave of my Mother, never expecting to see her more."

But even at death Washington's resentment at the financial burden he carried for his mother had to be expressed. "She has had a great deal of money from me at times . . . and over and above this has not only had all that ever was made from the plantation but got her provisions and everything else she thought proper from thence. In short, to the best of my recollection I have never in my life received a copper from the estate, and have paid many hundred pounds (first and last) to her in cash. However, I want no retribution. I conceived it to be a duty whenever she asked for money, and I had it, to furnish her notwithstanding she got all the crops or the amount of them, and took everything she wanted from the plantation for the support of her family, horses &c besides."

Years later George Washington Parke Custis summed up the tempestuous relationship between Mary Ball Washington and her oldest son. "[She] seemed to say, 'I am your mother, the being who gave you life, the guide who directed your steps when they needed the guidance of age and wisdom, the parental affection which claimed your love, the parental authority which commanded your obedience; whatever may be your success, whatever your reknown, next to your God you owe them most to me.'"

Lawrence Washington, George's half-brother, by an unknown English
artist, *c.* 1738. Lawrence was probably in school in England when this
portrait was painted. MOUNT VERNON LADIES' ASSOCIATION

Martha Washington, by Charles Willson Peale, 1772. George carried this miniature of Martha with him during the war. MOUNT VERNON LADIES' ASSOCIATION

George Washington, by Charles Willson Peale, 1772. This is the earliest known portrait of George. WASHINGTON AND LEE UNIVERSITY

John (Jacky) Parke Custis, by Charles Willson Peale, 1772. MOUNT VERNON LADIES' ASSOCIATION

Martha (Patsy) Parke Custis, by Charles Willson Peale, 1772. MOUNT VERNON LADIES' ASSOCIATION

Eleanor (Nelly) Parke Custis, by Robert Edge Pine, 1785. MOUNT VERNON LADIES' ASSOCIATION

George Washington Parke Custis, by Robert Edge Pine, 1785. WASHINGTON AND LEE UNIVERSITY

Nelly and Patty were eight and six; Wash and Betsey were four and nine when Pine painted their portraits.

Elizabeth (Betsey) Parke Custis, by Robert Edge Pine, 1785. WASHINGTON AND LEE UNIVERSITY

Martha (Patty) Parke Custis, by Robert Edge Pine, 1785. MOUNT VERNON LADIES' ASSOCIATION

George's nephew Bushrod Washington, by Henry Benbridge, Philadelphia, 1783. Bushrod, oldest son of John Augustine Washington, inherited Mount Vernon. MOUNT VERNON LADIES' ASSOCIATION

Frances (Fanny) Bassett, by Robert Edge Pine, 1785. Martha's niece
Fanny married George's nephew George Augustine Washington. MOUNT
VERNON LADIES' ASSOCIATION

Eleanor (Nelly) Parke Custis, by James Sharples, Philadelphia, c. 1796.
Nelly was a much-admired seventeen when this portrait was made.

George Washington Parke Custis, by Charles B. J. F. De Saint-Memin, 1808. At twenty-seven Wash was no longer a moody adolescent. ROBERT E. LEE, IV

George Washington, by Jean Antoine Houdon, 1785. His family thought this was the best likeness of the president. MOUNT VERNON LADIES' ASSO-CIATION

IV

THE PRESIDENCY

1789–1797

"Awful As A God . . .
Most Affectionate of Fathers"

*T*he departure by carriage of the president's immediate family from Mount Vernon for New York in May, 1789, was a teary one, according to escort Bob Lewis. "Servants of the House, and a number of the field negroes . . . greatly affected. . . . My aunt equally so." Left behind with George Augustine and Fanny and their young children was Sam's orphan, Harriot Washington.

Martha, ten-year-old Nelly, eight-year-old Wash, and their servants stopped for the night at Abingdon to say goodbye to Nelly Stuart and the older Custis girls. They left at 5 A.M. the next day with "the family in tears the children a bawling."

Near Baltimore the carriage boarded Hammond's Ferry to cross a stretch of water. High wind and waves frightened Martha, but at Mrs. Carroll's mansion on the other side she was refreshed by iced punch. The party consumed two gallons in fifteen minutes, Bob recorded in his journal.

The children were "very well and cheerfull all the way." Nelly complained a "very little of being sick," Martha wrote Fanny later. At Baltimore fireworks and a band which serenaded Martha until 2 A.M. contributed to the excitement. In Philadelphia crowds greeted the new president's family, bells rang, and a thirteen-gun salute was fired. Martha slipped away to Mr. Whiteside's fancy drygoods shop to buy "new fashioned" shoes for the female relatives she'd left behind, a doll for Fanny's little Maria, painting and drawing materials for granddaughters Betsey and Patty.

Washington and a barge were waiting at Elizabethtown Point, New Jersey, to carry the tired but exhilarated travelers the fifteen miles across Upper New York Bay to New York City. Thirteen oarsmen rowed a steady course through the boats of welcoming onlookers that surrounded the barge. "Dear little Washington seemed to be lost in a mase at the great parade that was made for us all the way we come."

At the small presidential house on Cherry and Queen Streets the Washingtons and their grandchildren occupied the second floor. Secretary-aides David Humphreys, nephew Bob Lewis, and Thomas Nelson shared a crowded room on the third floor, where Humphreys was wont to recite poetry in the middle of the night to his long-suffering roommates. Nelly "is a little wild creature and spends her time at the window looking at carriages, etc. passing by—which is new to her and very common for children to do," Martha wrote Fanny.

The first lady's hair was set and dressed daily. "You would I fear think me a good deal in the fashion if you could but see me." The servants were clothed in white and scarlet livery, and a New York chef prepared elegant meals. Sixteen horses were curried and groomed under the watchful eyes of Bishop, master of the stables.

The president held weekly afternoon levees for properly attired and comported gentlemen who cared to attend. The first lady held a reception Fridays for both gentlemen and ladies—"similar but more sociable." Vice-President John

Adams's wife Abigail described the levees to her sister. "The form of Reception is this, the servants announce and Col. Humphries or Mr. Lear, receives every Lady at the door, and Hands her up to Mrs. Washington to whom she makes a most Respectfull courtesy and then is seated without noticeing any of the rest of the company. The President then comes up and speaks to the Lady, which he does with a grace dignity and ease, that leaves Royal George far behind him."[18] "All the chairs are occupied by the Ladies, and the floor by the Gentlemen, who stand up," Bob Lewis wrote his mother.

Martha was not stiff, Abigail made clear to her sister. "Mrs. Washington is a most friendly, good Lady, always pleasent & easy, doatingly fond of her Grandchildren, to whom she is quite the Grandmamma. . . . She is plain in her dress, but that plainness is the best of every article. . . . Her manners are modest and unassuming, dignified and femenine . . . no lady can be more deservedly beloved and esteemed as she is. . . . I found myself much more deeply impressed than I ever did before their Majesties of Britain."[19] "Mrs. Washington is certainly one of the most agreeable ladies of the whole world," wrote one observer. "Her little grandchildren are very promising. . . . the President is as awful as a God." "Mrs. Washington is the very essence of kindness," said another. "[Her] hospitality seems to nearly spread over the whole place."

"My first care," wrote Martha, "was to get the children to a good school,—which they are boath very much pleased at." As the weeks went by, they must have been less pleased. At the end of the year Nelly was reenrolled in a Mrs. Graham's school on Maiden Lane, and Wash began studying (along with seven other boys) with a Mr. Murdock. Mr. Dunlop was engaged for drawing and painting lessons for Nelly. Music teacher Alexander gave demanding lessons on the new pianoforte Washington bought. Nelly "played

18. Abigail Adams, *New Letters of Abigail Adams* (Boston, 1971), p. 19.
19. Ibid., pp. 13, 15, 30, 57.

and cried and cried and played," her brother wrote years later. Into her French exercise book Nelly copied her daily schedule. "Mondays—Get some French by heart. Rehearse the last two grammar lessons.

"Wednesdays & Fridays—Get one page of Diologues; get ½ page of Grammar lessons.

"Tuesdays & Fridays—Get one page Dialogues.

"Saturdays—Be examined in the Dialogues and parse some French. Translate every day but Saturday."

Tobias Lear took the children to the theater and the "Natural Curiosities." Martha saw "The Speaking Image" (a large doll that answered questions), and the whole family went to church, the waxworks, and on coach rides to the country. In his *Recollections* Wash remembered theater audiences in the pit and gallery calling out for "Washington's March," and that at one of his grandmother's receptions "the ostrich feathers in the head-dress of Miss McIver caught fire from the Chandelier" and Major Jackson "clapped the fire out with his hands."

"The children are well and in way of improvement," Washington wrote Dr. Craik. The dignity of the first magistrate's household did not prevent childlike play. "Ball and marbles, a small cannon, a drum, skeats, paints" were purchased. The *Young Americans* was performed in the attic. Nelly remembered that her grandfather—"the most affectionate of fathers"—"laughed heartily at saucy descriptions of any scene in which she had taken part or any one." He delighted in Nelly's and her friends' "merry pranks," but his august presence created a reserve among her contemporaries that "they could not overcome." Washington wrote John Dandridge: "Miss Eleanor and Master Custis . . . desire that their Cousin may be informed that they are at very good schools and are extremely fond of them and the Companions which they meet there, but they cannot help wishing for a return of their happy hours at Mount Vernon."

Washington was desperately ill twice during the first years of his presidency. A rope was stretched across Cherry Street to keep carriages from passing by, straw was spread on the sidewalks to muffle footsteps, and vendors were not allowed to call out their wares. A few months after his first recovery the president took a tour of the New England states and Martha ("much indisposed since she came here") sank into a depression. "I live a very dull life here and know nothing that passes in the town—I never goe to any publick place—indeed I think I am more like a state prisoner than anything else, there is certain bounds set for me which I must not depart from—and as I cannot doe as I like I am obstinate and stay at home a great deal."[20]

A month later her mood had improved. Both she and her husband were pleased at the proofs of regard from their countrymen for the president, she wrote Mercy Warren. If younger, they would probably have enjoyed them more. Yet Martha would rather be home at Mount Vernon. "I do not say this because I feel dissatisfied with my present situation. No, God forbid! for every body and every thing conspire to make me as contented as possible in it yet I know too much from the splendid scenes of public life. I am still determined to be cheerful and to be happy, in whatever situation I may be; for I have also learned from experience that the greatest part of our happiness or misery depends upon our dispositions, and not upon our circumstances. We carry the seeds of the one or the other about with us, in our minds, wherever we go."

The following June Martha wrote Mercy Warren another introspective letter. "I continue to be as happy hear as I could be at any place except Mount Vernon. My grandchildren have . . . as good opportunities for acquiring a useful and accomplished education. In their happiness, my own is, in a great measure, involved. . . . If Congress should have a recess this summer . . . I hope to go home to Mount Vernon for a few months; and from that expectation I already derive much comfort."

Martha was happiest when she was doing what she did

20. Original letter owned by Pennsylvania Historical Society.

best—staying at home supervising her portion of the running of Mount Vernon. Plantation responsibilities were still shared with the president, however, as shown by his long letters to nephew George Augustine and subsequent managers. "Mrs. Washington requested the Gardeners Wife . . . to superintend . . . the care of the Spinners. . . . Mrs. Washington desires you will order the Ashes to be taken care of, that there may be no want of Soap . . . under cover with this letter you will receive some Lima Beans which Mrs. Washington desires may be given to the Gardener. . . . Mrs. Washington desires you will direct Old Doll to distil a good deal of Rose and Mint Water & ca.; and we wish to know whether the Linnen for the People is all made up? . . . Charlotte at the Mansion House has been reported sick for several weeks. Mrs. Washington desires you will examine her case, and if it appears necessary to request Dr. Craik to attend, and prescribe for her." "I am truly sorry to hear of another death in the [slave] family so soon," Martha wrote Fanny.

She still depended on Mount Vernon to provide some food and services for the well-ordered running of the presidential household. "Mrs. Washington desires you will send her by the first Vessel to this place one dozn of the best Hams & half a dozn. Midlings of Bacon . . . requests that the Gardner would send her some Artichoke seeds . . . expected two barrels of *good* Shad would have come round with the things which were sent from Mount Vernon." "I send by Hercules some rufles for my little Boys bosom which I beg you will make Charlotte hem," Martha wrote Fanny ". . . and whip them ready to sew on and send me six at a time as his old ruffles are worne to raggs."

The Virginia relatives were never far from Martha's tender heart, as the letters to Fanny demonstrate. "I wish you to take a prayer book for yourself and give one to Hariot the other two to be given to Betty and Patty Custis . . . when you write your Brother [Burwell, Jr.] remember me affectionately to them." Martha wished Burwell's wife would look after niece Patty Dandridge. "I have a great regard for her and wish to see her do well . . . give sweet little Maria a thousand kisses for me I often think of the dear little engaging child—and wish her with me to hear her little prattle. . . . You must let me know if you in a certain way and when the event will happen, as it must be very inconvenient to you for us to come home about the time . . . my love and good wishes attend you and all with you."

Early in 1790 Washington gave his presidential message to Congress and at the same time gave a boost to the nation's manufacturing industry. "On this occasion I was dressed in a suit of clothes made at the woolen manufactury at Hartford, as the buttons also were." (Ordered for Martha in May was "Hartford brown cloth" for a riding dress.) Secretary of the Treasury Alexander Hamilton presented a proposal for paying war debts, which inspired the first controversy within the fledgling administration.

Overcrowded conditions in the presidential house were getting on the nerves of Washington and his family. In February they moved to a larger house on Broadway with a view of the Hudson. We "long to enjoy our own [fireside] at Mount Vernon," the president wrote Mrs. Graham. But he and his wife had precedents to establish. "I think our plans of living will now be deemed reasonable by the considerate part of our species." The Washingtons' perceptions of presidential style were harmonious. "Her [Mrs. Washington's] wishes coincide with my own as to simplicity of dress."

In August twenty-nine Creek Indians were entertained at the executive mansion and a peace treaty signed with them. In the fall the president felt free enough from business to take his family to Mount Vernon for two months before returning in the late fall to the new seat of government, Philadelphia. Mr. Lear and his bride Polly ("a pretty spritely woman") were to prepare the executive mansion on High Street and find schools for the grandchildren. Martha feared that in Philadelphia they "would not enjoy so many advantages to the point of education" as in New York, Martha wrote Mercy Warren. Wash's grandfather instructed Lear: "Use your best endeavors to ascertain the characters, or reputation of such Schools as it may be proper to place Washington at . . . particularly if there be any fit School in the College for him, under good and able Tutors, and well attended. His trip to Mount Vernon will be of no Service to him, but will render restraint more necessary than ever."

Philadelphia was as gay as New York. Mr. Lear took the children to Mr. Peale's Museum, and Nelly had a silver-threaded and espangled dress for Mr. Robardet's dancing school. The president and his wife were carried to the theater and Assembly balls in a cream-colored coach with painted panels representing the four seasons, drawn by six cream-colored horses.

Congress adjourned in March, 1791, after creating the Bank of the U.S. which was supported by Washington's secretary of the treasury, Alexander Hamilton, and opposed by his secretary of state, Thomas Jefferson. The president left for a long tour of the southern states, and his wife missed him. "I have never heard from the President since he left Mount Vernon," she wrote Fanny wistfully. A letter from Washington to Lear instructed him to "furnish Mrs. Washington with what money she may want, and from time to time ask her if she does want, as she is not fond of applying."

Although a geography book, cyphering book, Erasmus, and Telemachus had been purchased for Wash, his schooling was not working out. Were the masters incompetent? "Colo. Hamilton, Gen'l Knox and the Attorney General have sons in the same predicament," Washington wrote Lear. He should "consult and act in Concert with them."

The trustees of the school had set up a committee to investigate "the mode in which the boys were instructed," Lear replied. They said they were obliged for the prod, but Lear had been told by others that they were "not pleased with my meddling." Washington was indignant. "It is hardly to be expected by the Trustees of *any* College, that complaints will not be made by the parents of friends of the boys who go to it, if they conceive they are neglected; and if Trustees mean to do their duty, and support the reputation of the Seminary, they ought, I am sure, to be thankful for well founded representations of neglect in the oeconomy, police, or inattention of the professors and teachers."

At about the same time Lear wrote former aide David Humphreys, now minister to Portugal, a frank appraisal of the Washington grandchildren. "Nelly and Washington have every advantage in point of instructors that this country can give them, and they certainly make good progress in those things which are taught them. But I apprehend the worst consequences particularly to the boy, from the unbounded indulgence of his grandmama. The ideas which are insinuated to him at home . . . that he is born to such noble properties both in estate and otherwise . . . and the servile respect the servants are obliged to pay to him . . . he is on the road to ruin." Washington refused to interfere.

"Betty and Patty are fine girls," Lear went on. Dr. Stuart had recently moved the family from Abingdon on the Potomac twenty miles inland to Hope Park. "I think it is much to be lamented that they and their very agreeable mother should be so much secluded from society."

Tobias Lear kept in touch with Nelly Custis Stuart, sending her reports on Nelly and Wash. "Your letters come like drops of rain from a cloud in a dry season," she told him. Nelly concurred with Lear's apprehension. "It gives me unfeined satisfaction to be informed my good Mama . . . has at last seen the necessity of making the Dr. children respect as well as love her, for that they never would have done had she continued her former improper indulgence to them." Nelly added wistfully: "I often lament my Dr Bett and Patt cannot have the same advantages . . . shake hands with my Dear Boy . . . don't let him forget he has a mother." Yet Nelly Stuart was "much alarmed" about her daughter and namesake. ". . . from her letters lately to her Sisters she appears too much engaged in dissipation. My Dear little child will I much fear be soon an affected, trifling Miss of the to[w]n."

During the president's long absence in the south the birth of Benjamin Lincoln Lear cheered the family left behind. "Many express their surprise," wrote independent New Hampshireman Lear, "that a son of mine born too in this family, should receive any other name than that of George Washington. But although I love and respect the great man who bears that name, yet I would not for the world do a thing that would savor of adulation toward him." Nelly celebrated her twelfth birthday, Wash his tenth, and Martha her sixtieth.

The "great man" returned July 6 as bank speculators were snatching up shares in the new national bank. The French revolutionary government broke its commercial treaty with the U.S. by putting a duty on tobacco and whale oil. The president learned that Louis XVI and Marie Antoinette had fled, intending to raise foreign armies to attack the French government. They had been caught and returned to Paris virtually as prisoners under the orders of Lafayette. Washington was distressed by this event, which spoiled France's relatively peaceful efforts toward reform.

The following February, 1792 the country celebrated Washington's sixtieth birthday. Tobias Lear wished the celebration "could make George Washington one year younger each year for many years to come." Because of a misunderstanding between Pierre L'Enfant, designer of the new federal city, and the commissioners, Washington had had to request his resignation. The president had done everything he could to retain L'Enfant, Lear wrote Humphreys, but the man had a "hasty, ungovernable temper." The previous Thursday Washington had for the first time exercised the veto—"the power of negating laws which the Constitution gives him."

His son Lincoln "runs alone," Lear wrote with pleasure. But the Washington grandchildren still worried him. They were "not taught to find resource in themselves for happiness." Lear feared that their grandmother "will experience many sorrowful hours on their accounts when the effects of her blind indulgence of them comes to display itself more fully—every day produces sad proofs of its evil tendency."

Why did George Washington—wise in so many ways—indulge his wife in her fatal flaw? "Mrs. Washington's happiness is bound up in the boy [Wash]. Any rigidity used towards him would perhaps be productive of grievous effects on her," the President explained to Lear. The question remains unanswered. As Lear predicted, the spoiling of Wash would bring "many sorrowful hours."

"Submit with Patience and Resignation"

The visits to Mount Vernon were becoming increasingly sad. Nephew George Augustine Washington was dying. In the fall of 1791 he had gone "over the mountains for his health," wrote his uncle . . . was "much better than he was, but not yet free from the pain in his breast and Cough." The following summer, while Washington also worried over Indian, British, and Spanish troubles on the frontier, citizen resistance to the excise tax on whisky, the growing animosity between cabinet members Hamilton and Jefferson, and whether to run again for the presidency, his nephew's situation was "unpromising and precarious, growing worse. Poor fellow!" George Augustine himself confirmed the analysis. "My health which is really so precarious that I am at a loss what to say about it. . . . Your truly affectionate nephew." In September— "Poor George! He is but a shadow of what he was."

In October, 1792 Fanny took her sick husband and three

young children home to her father, Burwell Bassett, at Eltham. Harriot Washington was sent to her aunt Betty Lewis in Fredericksburg. Fanny's father would not live long himself. A fall from a horse caused injuries from which he could not recover. On January 20, 1793 Washington wrote Governor Henry Lee. "I am sorry to be informed by your letter that death has snatched fro us my old acquaintance and friend, Colo. Bassett. The manner of it, adds to the regret. We shall all follow, some sooner and some later; and, from accounts, my poor Nephew is likely to be among the first."

A week later Washington wrote that nephew: "My dear George—I do not write to you often, because I have no business to write upon, because all the News I could communicate is contained in the Papers which I forward every week; because I conceive it unnecessary to repeat the assurances of sincere regard and friendship I have always professed for you, or the disposition I feel to render every Service in my power to you and yours; and lastly because I conceive the more undisturbed you are, the better it is for you.

"It has given your friends much pain to find that change of Air has not been productive of that favorable change in your health, which was the wishes of them all. But the will of Heaven is not to be controverted or scrutinized by the children of this world. It therefore becomes the Creatures of it to submit with patience and resignation to the will of the Creator whether it be to prolong, or to shorten the number of our days. To bless them with health, or afflict them with pain.

"My fervent wishes attend you, in which I am heartily joined by your Aunt, and these are extended with equal sincerity to Fanny and the Children. I am always your Affecte. Uncle."

"The President and myself feel very sincerely for you in your heavy afflictions," Martha told Fanny. Two weeks later it was all over. February 24, 1793, George Washington to Fanny Washington: "To you, who so well know the affectionate regard I had for our departed friend, it is unnecessary to describe the sorrow with which I was afflicted at the news of his death. . . . The object of the present letter is to convey to your mind the warmest assurances of my love, friendship, and disposition to serve you; These also I profess to have in an eminent degree, for your Children."

March 4, 1793, the day of Washington's unwished-for second inauguration, was a troubled one for the president. Word had come that Lafayette was imprisoned in Austria, the victim of further upheavals in France. The February packet had brought news of war between France and England. "The great question now seems to be," wrote Lear, "what course shall the United States steer to keep themselves from being involved in the contest." Washington's recent birthday celebrations, even the levees, were the object of criticism by the Republican press as royal pomp. And he had lost both his brother-in-law and beloved nephew.

George Augustine had been building a house for his family on the property his uncle had given him. When he died, Washington ordered construction halted, but offered Fanny continuing residence at Mount Vernon. Fanny wondered if it wouldn't be "best for me to live in Alexandria . . . in a small town house that I could there attend particularly to the education of my children," but wanted her uncle's advice. "The offer of a residence at Mount Vernon," Washington replied, "was made to you with my whole heart, but it is with you to consider nevertheless whether any other plan will comport better with the views which my Nephew had, or with such as you may have entertained for your own ease, for the education of your Children; or for the interest of the Estate."

In time Fanny and her children did move to Washington's house in Alexandria. In spite of a multiplicity of calls on his attention the president continued to look out for her. "I shall always be sincerely disposed to give you my opinion upon any, and every point you may desire respecting the management of your Estate, or the Children . . . it is my wish that you would never be backward in laying them before me."

"If Mrs. Fanny Washington does not draw a Sein at her own landing . . . let her get what she wants at my landing; and at any rate . . . always send some [fish] for her table." Fanny sent "every sentiment of gratitude, respect and affection . . . my children desire me to present their love to you."

The summer after George Augustine's death Philadelphia and other cities seethed with the agitation of pro-French citizens roused by new French Minister Genet. Washington had tried to keep America out of France's wars with other countries with a Proclamation of Neutrality in April. But that summer "Washington's home was surrounded by an innumerable multitude, from day to day huzzahing, demanding war against England, cursing Washington, and crying success to the French patriots."[21] Soon a yellow fever epidemic drove the mobs inside, and took a life in the president's own household—young Polly Lear . . . "a woman so amiable and pleasing in her manners."

Her grieving husband took off for Europe on a commercial errand, leaving Lincoln with his mother in New Hampshire. "Our little favorite," Washington called him when writing Lear. "We sincerely wish . . . he may always be as charming and promising as he now is." His godfather had sent him a lottery ticket for the hotel to be built in the new federal city on the Potomac, and was amused when Lincoln "declared if his Ticket should turn up a prize he would go to live in the Federal City. . . . Mrs. Washington . . . desires me to assure you of her sincere love for him in which I join and of her friendship and regard for you. In whatever place you may be or in whatever walk of life you may move my best wishes will attend you, for I am, and always shall be your sincere friend & c."

In August, 1794 Lear returned to Georgetown with a "valuable cargo of Goods." A letter from "your good mother to Mrs. Washington [reported] that she, and little Lincoln were perfectly well," Washington wrote Lear from Phila-

21. Freeman, *George Washington* VII, p. 119n.

delphia. "To see you, wd make this family happy." It must
have made them even happier when not long afterward
Lear married Fanny. Washington promptly gave them a
life lease on a house and 360 acres of his Mount Vernon
estate.

Martha Washington had friends in Philadelphia, enjoyed
her husband's company, and doted on her grandchildren.
("Nelly is a woman in size. Washington begins to be a sturdy
boy.") But with her niece Fanny there was a special bond.
A series of letters to Fanny from 1794–5 reveal both the
scope and limitations of the First Lady's interests and
experience.

January 14, 1794: ". . . all well not the least fear of yellow
fever while the weather is cold almost every family has lost
some of their friends the players are not allowed to come
here . . . no assembly."

February 10: ". . . very dull all winter a great number of
the people in this town is very much at a loss how to spend
their time agreeably . . . the gay are always fond of some
[thing] new."

March 2: "Patty [Custis] and Mr. Peter is to make a match
. . . the new French minister seems to be a plain grave and
good man . . . as far as we can judge from his looks and
manners he is a very agreeable man."

March 9: ". . . the girls and Mr. Peter are here for 5 weeks.
. . . Betsy may stay . . . the Congress is up and all the members gone home the President has some particular business
which will prevent his fixing a time as yet" (to go to Mount
Vernon).

England was threatening war on the frontier, seizing U.S.
ships, and impressing its seamen. Congress passed a thirty-
day embargo on foreign trade, and Supreme Court Justice
John Jay was nominated by the president as a special envoy
to Great Britain. Martha had other matters on her mind.

May 10: "Betsy you know is often complaining . . . no
time to work . . . stands at the window all day to look at
what is doing in the street. Betsy does not take much pleasure in going out to visit—great many visits to see her."

June 2: "The President thinks publick bsn. will keep him in this place all summer—and it would not be agreeable for me to stay at Mount Vernon without him."

June 15: Martha is sorry Fanny's daughter is ill. "I have not a doubt but worms, is the principle cause of her complaints. Children that eat everything that they like and feed as heartily as your does must be full of worms—Indeed my dear Fanny I never saw children stuffed as yours was and reather wondered that they were able to be tolerable with such lodes as they used to put into their little stomachs."

June 30: "Nelly has a toothache . . . subject to with colds . . . won't take care of self . . . a pore thoughtless child."

July 14: written from Germantown ". . . this fine airy place. The President is getting better fast. . . . [He is] pleased with Mr. Pearce's* management . . . will not I hope be so anxious about his plantation business." Nelly has returned "very much pleased with her jaunt."

August 3: Martha is "truly sorry for pore Mrs. Craik as she has several good children left she should endevor to reconcile herself to the loss of one however hard it may be.

"The President has had Doctor Tate to look at the spot on his face he makes light of the thing I trust in god that it will soon be perfectly well.

"Bart† sprained his shoulder . . . with other complaints . . . has been a good while a complaining—indeed my only motive for coming to this place was my hopes of its being servisable to the President, the children, and him."

September 15: In another attempt to be serviceable to her husband by freeing him from one responsibility, Martha advises her niece to "keep your matters in order yourself without depending on others as that is the only way to be happy I would rouse myself and not trouble any mortal I hope my dear Fanny you will look upon this advice in the friendly way it is meant—as I wish you to be as independent as your circumstance will admit."

September 29: "Phila.—hot sickly no schools but the col-

---

* the new Mount Vernon manager.

† Martha's nephew, a presidential aide.

lege . . . the little ones not attended at all. . . . Washington attends but doesn't learn."

After the house of the excise inspector in Pittsburgh, Pennsylvania, was burned by rebellious taxpayers, Washington empowered Secretary Hamilton to mobilize militia to quelch the "whiskey rebellion." The president himself rode to the rendezvous in western Maryland of troops from New Jersey, Pennsylvania, Maryland, and Virginia. Martha's nephew Bart Dandridge accompanied him, and Washington's nephew George Lewis, who was in command of Virginia horse-troops, was encountered enroute.

October 18: ". . . insurgents in back country. . . . President sent troops . . . not heard from P. since he left Carlyle."

November 11: "The Prs. has returned from westward . . . the spot on his face is gone. . . . Mr. Dandridge is better."

December 5: "Nelly not so much grown as Mr. L. describes. . . . Wash has outgrown clothes. I hope when Nelly has a little more gravitie she will be a good girl—at present—she is I fear half-crazy." ("Harum scaram sans soucie," Nelly described herself. The following fall she was sent to Virginia for the winter.)

April 5, 1795: "Betsy wishes to stay with me . . . very grave . . . wouldn't go to assembly with me and Nelly last week . . . nor church . . . not feeling well. . . . Miss Morris' wedding is next Thurs. the girls to go . . . expect to go to Mount Vernon the 14th."

By then a copy of Jay's treaty with Great Britain had arrived—a treaty which would cost George Washington severe criticism.

The following March there could be no more letters to Fanny. Betsy Custis sent the painful news of her death. Once again Martha was called upon to endure the loss of a close family member. "Mrs. Lear was good and amiable, and your Society will feel the loss of her," Washington wrote Betsy. To Tobias Lear he exposed the anguish in his own home and heart. "Your former letters prepared us for the stroke . . . ; but it has fallen heavily notwithstanding.

"It is the nature of humanity to mourn for the loss of our friends; and the more we loved them, the more poignant is our grief. . . . It is our duty to submit . . . But nature will, notwithstanding, indulge, for a while, its sorrows.

"To say how much we loved, and esteemed our departed friend, is unnecessary. She is now no more! but she must be happy, because her virtue has a claim to it.

"At all times, and under all circumstances, we are, and ever shall remain, Your sincere and Affectionate friends."

On the same day the president notified the House of Representatives of his unequivocal refusal on constitutional grounds to turn over executive documents concerning the controversial treaty Justice Jay had made with England.

Fanny's and George Augustine's children must be cared for. To Fanny's brother Washington wrote: "Mr. Lear is now in this city. At first, he seemed unwilling to part with any of them, but upon mature reflection yielded to the propriety of your having Maria. And as he has engaged a tutor, and was on the point of taking his own Son home, it was concluded that the boys [George Fayette and Charles Augustine] should remain with him until my re-establishment (next March) at Mount Vernon, when some New arrangement might be made.

"It had always been my intention . . . to take Fayette under my . . . care, but . . . it would be best . . . and more grateful to *their* feelings to keep them together. . . . The Children at present are all at Mount Vernon."

Lear's mother came down from New Hampshire to help care for the children. Eight-year-old Maria was a handful. Martha wrote to Mrs. Lear: "I was extremely sorry to be told . . . how ill she had behaved to you . . . had I known it before I should have reprimanded her very seriously—she has always been a spoiled child—as indeed they were all. I wish something may be done with her for her advantage. I loved the childs mother and I love her."

Maria's great-aunt and uncle did more than wring their hands. "The President sent Mr. Dandridge to enquire of the Minister of the Moravian Church if he could get Maria into the school at Bethlehem." The school is full, the minister reports, but "the President will wright to Bethlehem and endeavor if its possible to get her in." Meanwhile, Mr. Lear should send Maria to her uncle. "We cannot take the child in hear our Family is large."

The Reverend Mr. Von Vleck, head of the Moravian School for Young Ladies at Bethlehem, did agree to make a place for the president's grandniece, and needed to know how soon she could be there. "Answer punctually," Washington wrote Lear. The headmaster was "pressed by others" for admission of their daughter. "Receiving Maria may be considered as a favor (at this time)."

Maria undoubtedly had qualms about going so far from home. Might her cousin, the daughter of Colonel Ball, come too, Washington wrote Von Vleck December 7, the same day he gave his eighth annual address to Congress? "I *know* that many unsuccessful applications has been made for admission," he wrote again to Lear. January 13, 1797 he still "has heard nothing from you" about Maria and school. On June 14 from Mount Vernon Washington sent one last letter to Von Vleck. Maria was in a consumption and couldn't come. So her cousin would not be going to Bethlehem either.

While Maria's schooling occupied the family, a domestic matter of larger social significance intruded. Oney, a servant of whom Mrs. Washington was "particularly fond," had run away. Washington wrote the secretary of the treasury with a request that a customs collector try to apprehend her. There was no question but what she had allowed herself to be seduced. Mrs. Washington was indignant at "the ingratitude of the girl, who was often in the Chamber of Miss Custis . . . brought up and treated more like a child than a Servant." She had been seen in New York and then New Hampshire.

Two months later word came that Oney wished to return to Virginia. Her French seducer had left and she had "betaken herself to the needle" for support. In antislavery New Hampshire the matter was a delicate one for the southern president. Washington would take Oney back if compulsory means were not needed. Otherwise, she must be taken by force to Virginia or the federal city . . . unless that would cause a scene. Nothing should be done to "excite a mob or riot."

Early in his first term the president had politely but non-committally received a Quaker gentleman who urged the immediate abolition of slavery. "As it was a matter which might come before me for official decision I was not inclined to express any sentiments on the merits of the question before this should happen." By the end of the presidency Washington privately acknowledged that he was "well disposed . . . to the gradual abolition . . . of that description of People," but did not wish to reward Oney's unfaithfulness. Mount Vernon slaves were well fed and clothed and not subject to the lash, New Englander Tobias Lear once wrote a friend—*"but still they are slaves."*

"Dear Uncle"

*W*hile public duties weighed him down and farming needs tugged at his heart, George Washington never relaxed his attention to the children of his brothers and sisters.

Sam's boys were still very much in evidence. "It gives me great pleasure to hear," Washington wrote Dr. Craik the first year of his first term, "and I wish you to express it to them that my Nephews George and Lawrence Washington are attentive to their studies, and obedient to your orders and admonition." At the end of 1790, however, their uncle decided they were "doing but little in Alexandria having left the study of the Languages," and suggested firmly that they should come to the College at Philadelphia. They were "well disposed Youths, neither of them wanting capacity."

Dec. 5, 1790, George Washington to George Steptoe Washington: "After you and Lawrence have carefully perused and well considered the enclosed statement, I wish you to determine whether you will come or not . . . If you determine to come on, you had better do it immediately. But I must repeat . . . that you come with good dispositions and determined resolutions to conform to establishments and pursue your studies. Your aunt joins me in love to you both."

Dec. 19, 1790, George Washington to George Steptoe Washington: "From the tenor of your letter it does not appear that Lawrence is to come on to this place with you, for he is not mentioned in any part of the letter. It is my intention that you should both enter the College together."

The needs of college-aged, gentlemanly nephews were not inexpensive. Books, paper and quills, board, mending and washing, firewood, clothes, violin and music master, theater tickets, dressing hair, watch with chain and seal, Assembly, and pocket money for George Steptoe and Lawrence appear subsequently as items in Washington's account books. In April, 1792 the brothers received diplomas from the College. In May they entered "the french school," and in June Mr. Edmund Randolph was paid "for receiving G.S. and L. to study the law." Tobias Lear was favorably impressed with Sam's sons. "They bid fair to become good and useful men."

There is no record in George Washington's *Writings* of his reaction to the news a few years later that George Steptoe had eloped to his father's run-down estate Harewood in Berkeley County, Virginia, with fifteen-year-old Lucy Payne (Dolley Madison's sister).

Lawrence went on with the study of law, but in 1794 asked his uncle for permission to leave expensive Philadelphia and study law in Berkeley. "I never excelled in professions of gratitude and respect," Lawrence wrote. "I shall only say that I feel more than I could possibly describe."

"I am My Dear Uncle your Sincere Niece." Correspondence with and about Harriot Washington, George Steptoe's and Lawrence's sister, tells a pathetic but somewhat comic story. It begins just before the presidency when Harriot was thirteen. She had been left at Mount Vernon under Fanny Washington's care.

March 31, 1789, George Washington to George A. Washington: "As I know of no resource that Harriot has for Supplies but from me, Fanny will, from time to time as occasion may require have such things got for her. . . . Mrs. Washington will I expect, leave her tolerably well provided with common articles for the present."

April 2, 1790, Harriot Washington to George Washington: "I will set down to write my dear Uncle as I have not written to him since he left this place. I should have done sooner but I thought you had so much business that I had better write to Aunt Washington, yet I am sure you would be very glad to see me improving myself by writing letters to my friends. I am a-going to ask you my dear Uncle to do something for me which I hope you will not be against, but I am sure if you are it will be for my good. As all the young ladies are a-learning music, I will be very much obliged to you if you will send me a gettar. There is a man here by the name of Tracy that teaches to play on the harpsichord and gettar. A gettar is so simple an instrument that five or six lessons would be sufficient for anybody to learn. If you think it proper to send me a gettar I will thank you if you will send it by the first opportunity. I was informed the other day that you and Aunt Washington were certainly a-coming home this summer, which gives me a great deal of pleasure for I want to see you very much. If you please to give my love to Aunt Washington, Nelly and Washington, I am dear Uncle your sincere niece, Harriot Washington."[22]

During his visit home Washington was not altogether pleased with Harriot. He wrote Tobias Lear, October 10, 1789: "The easy and quiet temper of Fanny is little fitted I find for the care of my Niece Harriot Washington, who is grown almost, is not quite a Woman; and what to do with her at the advanced *Size* she is arrived at, I am really at a loss. Her age (just turned of 14) is not too great for a

22. Original letter owned by the Massachusetts Historical Society.

Boarding School, but to enter now with any tolerable prospect, the Mistress of it must not only be respectable, but one who establishes and will enforce good rules. She is prone to idleness, and having been under no control, would create all the difficulty." Was there "a *proper* School in Philadelphia (for her to board at) [with] genteel girls of her size and age? . . . I have not intimated any thing of this matter to Harriot yet; who, if it should be, would I dare say be a good deal alarmed."

Harriot stayed in Virginia. A year later the president sent her a typical Uncle Washington letter. October, 30, 1791, "I have received your letter, and shall always be glad to hear from you. . . . Occupied as my time is, and must be during the sitting of Congress, I nevertheless will endeavor to inculcate upon your mind the delicacy and danger of that period, to which you are now arrived under peculiar circumstances. You are just entering into the state of womanhood, without the watchful eye of a Mother to admonish, or the protecting aid of a Father to advise and defend you; you may not be sensible that you are at this moment about to be stamped with that character which will adhere to you through life; the consequence of which you have not perhaps attended to, but be assured it is of the utmost importance that you should."

Harriot was more interested in the guitar. By the following spring there was still no sign of it. May 28, 1792, "If my dear Uncle finds, it convenient to give me a guittar. . . . I should not trouble you . . . if I was not certain that I could learn myself . . . but Mrs. Bushrod Washington has been so kind as to offer to teach me, if I could not learn myself."

In July Martha wrote Fanny, "The President has given Miss Harriot a guitarre."[23] It was on a vessel bound for Mount Vernon.

The fall of 1792, when Fanny took her sick husband and children home to Eltham, Washington asked his sister Betty if she would take their niece. Betty replied:

"I shall have no objection to her being with me, if she

23. Original letter owned by Joseph Fields.

comes well cloathed or Provided to get them, that she may appear tolerable for I can assure you it was not so while with me before, by which means she was prevented frequently from appearing in publick, when it would have been my wish she should."

This would not happen again, George assured his sister. "She comes, as Mrs. Washington informs me, very well provided with everything proper for a girl in her situation: this much I know, that she costs me enough to place her in it. . . . Harriot has sense enough, but no disposition to industry, nor to be careful of her clothes. . . . I wish you would examine her clothes and direct her in their use and application of them; for without this they will be, I am told, dabbed about in every hole and corner, and her best things always in use. Fanny was too easy . . . and Mrs. Washington's absence has been injurious to her in many respects; but she is young, and with good advice may yet make a fine woman."

By February of the next year George was referring happily to "my niece Harriot Washington . . . whose conduct I hear with pleasure, has given much satisfaction to my sister." But during the fall of 1793 the needs of Betty's own family were so pressing she could no longer afford to keep Harriot. George instructed Lear to accept one hundred pounds for a quitclaim. The money was to be sent "for her immediate support" to "my Brothers only daughter (who from the involved State of his affairs, had left her by his Will a very small pittance; and the obtainment of that, even doubtful.)" Betty agreed to keep their niece.

The trouble was that Harriot (with her Washington genes) kept growing.

Jan. 7, 1794, Harriot Washington to George Washington: ". . . the only Freind, on earth that I can apply to for any thing." She wants money for a silk jacket and shoes for the birth night ball . . . "the first Ball I shall have been to this winter."

Feb. 3, 1794, Betty Lewis to George Washington: Harriot is pleased with the present. "She values it more as it

January the 29: 1793

My Dear Brother

Your letters of June the 6: and 14: of this month came duly to hand, the enclosed letter to my son Robert met with a speedy conveyance the same day, the other with the Money for Harriet, which I shall see that no part of it shall be laid out but in those things that is really necessary, it is unfortunate for her my living in Town for many things that could be wore to the last string in a Cuntry Place, will not do here, where we see so much Company, I must say less would be more agreeable to me,

I must in Justice to Harriet say she Pays the strictest regard to the advice I give her and really she is very Ingenious in makeing Clothes and altering them to the best advantage, your letter of the 6. should have receiv'd an earlier acknowledgment but my haveing buisiness in Town to sell what little Wheat I had made, my letter was not sent as I directed, I wish Howell to give me some information what it sells for in Philadelphia and if it will rise or fall in the Price — Harriet desires me to thank you for your Kindness to her, and joins me in returning your Compliment, by wishing you many happy New Years

I am with sincear love to you and my sister
Your Affet. Sister Betty Lewis

comes from Philadelphia and Expects it is more fashionable. I can assure you she is truly deserving of the favors receiv'd, I am not acquainted with any one who takes more cear of there things and turns them to greater advantage."

March 5, 1794, Harriot Washington to George Washington: She wants money for a "peice of linnen, some dimmity to make me petticoats and a great coat. . . . I have not had a great coat since, the winter I spent at Shootershill, mine is not entirely worn out, but it is so small that I cant get it on."

May 25, 1794, Harriot Washington to George Washington: From Harewood, where she is visiting her brother and his bride. Harriot is pleased with her "sister." Mrs. Dolley Madison is there too and has invited Harriot to visit the Madisons in Philadelphia. Might she have her uncle's permission to do so? Mrs. Madison is "a charming woman" to whom Harriot is "very much attached indeed."

In the spring of 1796 another sort of permission was being sought. A certain Andrew Parks wished to marry Harriot. He "is respected, sober, sedate, attentive to bsn." Betty wrote her brother. Washington sought more information. "Harriot haveing very little fortune herself, has no *right* to expect a great one in the man she marry's; but if he has not a competency to support her in the way she has lived, in the circle of her friends, she will not find the matrimonial state so comfortable as she may have expected when a family is looking up to her and but scanty means to support it."

Are Parks's connections respectable? Betty has sent no account of his family—native or a foreigner? Parks is a man in trade. Does he have any property?

"I do not wish to thwart Harriots inclination. . . . I should have preferred that she shd have remained single until I was once more settled at Mount Vernon . . . because then she would have been in the way of seeing much company and would have had a much fairer prospect."

Betty's son George Lewis looked into the matter of Parks's assets, found them lacking, and thought the match would be "extreme madness." Harriot's cousin Lawrence made some inquiries and came to a different conclusion. He sent his best wishes, Betty reported to George in June. "Harriot is not well. I believe her anxiety for fear of offending and not gaining your consent has Produc'd this, your long Silence has given her much uneasiness." Betty thought it high time her brother sent his blessing. "I think Harriot is Old Enougf now to make choice for her self, and if they are not happy I believe it will be her one falt, he bars the Best caracter of any young Person that I know." Besides, Betty had plans of her own. July 17, 1796, Harriot Washington Parks to George Washington: She is obliged for the one hundred dollars he has given her for "wedding cloaths . . . also a great deal of good advice." Her uncle has shown "great goodness and attention to me. And if my Uncle will only answer my letter and say he is not offended at my union (which took place yesterday, Aunt Lewis going immediately to Berkeley Co. to stay until the fall, and finding it not convenient to carry me with her, wished us married before she went). I shall be happy, for after my dear Uncle's protection and kindness to me I should be a most miserable being to reflect that I had displeased my greatest friend."

There is no record of a reply from Washington. But Martha sent a gift of earrings. And the diaries show that Harriot and Andrew Parks were welcomed to Mount Vernon in September, 1798.

John and Hannah Washington's sons, Bushrod and Corbin, were less of a problem and remained dear to their uncle's heart. "Among the first acts of my recommencing business (after lying six weeks on my right side) is that of writing you," Washington told Bushrod after one serious illness during the presidency. Although he might have wished to, "your standing at the bar would not justify my nominating you as Attorney to the Federal district Court in preference of some of the oldest, and most esteemed General Court Lawyers in your own State. . . . My political

conduct in nominations . . . must be exceedingly circum-
spect and proof against just criticism. . . . love to yourself
and Nancy."

Corbin asked for help over a land title dispute. Washington was sorry, but he had no "papers in my possession . . .
which can throw any light on the matter." He could not
resist a little advice. "It is the last time, probably, I shall
ever express any sentiment to you upon the occasion. . . .
Your Aunt joins me in best wishes for you and I am Dear
Corbin Your Affecte. friend & Uncle."

February 8, 1793, George Washington to Bushrod
Washington: "I am sorry to think I have cause to accuse
you of inattention to my requests. I have not heard a word
from you." But a year later: "It gives me much pleasure to
hear, through a variety of channels, that you are becoming
eminent and respectable in the Law."

In 1798 President John Adams appointed thirty-six-year-
old Bushrod a Supreme Court justice.

Whenever possible, Washington hired family members
as personal assistants. Bartholomew Dandridge, Jr., a
twenty-one-year-old fatherless nephew of Martha's had
come to the presidential household in 1793 to take Tobias
Lear's place as private secretary. He shared a room with
Wash. Lear sent David Humphreys a description of him.
". . . a young gentleman of an excellent mind strong
natural parts, 'tho but little acquainted with the world—his
education has been very limited, but his talent for improvement is great and his industry equal to it—he will
make a valueable and useful man."

Not even a busy president can be indifferent to the quirks
and emotions of an intimate relation. In the spring of 1796
Dandridge suddenly left "without a moment's intimation."
He returned but disappeared again in July. Washington
wrote a worried letter to Bart's brother John Dandridge.
"Your brother Bart['s] conduct is too enigmatical for me to
develope . . . his sudden and abrupt departure, was not
occasioned by any difference between us." Four days later

a letter came "intimating that when he was more composed, he would write me more fully, and give some explanation of his conduct. A Second and a third letter has been
received from him since without doing this." He wants to
return but cannot . . . "another Gentn. has taken his place.
If however I can render him any service I shall do it chear-
fully, as I have always entertained and continue to entertain a favourable opinion of his integrity and abilities. P.S.
your brother Bar arrived here . . . he is writing to you."
Washington either ignored or forgot the letters Bart had
written him previously in which he expressed a desire to
resign because he wanted "a small farm in the upper country of Virginia." There was "not one office (in the next
Administration) wch I would accept upon the condition of
residing longer in this city."

A spicy and apparently innacurate speculation of Bart's
behavior is found in John Adams's diary. July 17, 1796,
"Anecdotes of Dandridge, and Mrs. W.'s Negro Woman.
Both disappeared—never heard of—know not where they
are."[24]

Bart was rehired after all for the rest of his uncle's term.
August 1 Washington wrote the secretary of war: "Mr.
Dandridge, who has rejoined my family. . . . As he left my
family a little suddenly, I thought it necessary to mention
this matter to you, lest *that* circumstance should be ascribed
to unworthy motives, none of which I have to charge him
with." There were no hard feelings. Back at Mount Vernon
after his retirement Washington wrote Bart a warm, generous letter of recommendation. The young man ate his
words about a new appointment and accepted one from
President Adams as minister to the Hague.

Sam's children . . . John's boys . . . Martha's nephew . . .
Betty's pack of boys. There seems to be no end to Washington's deserving nephews. Perhaps it was compassion that
caused him to educate, admonish, and employ them. And

24. John Adams, *Diary and Autobiography* III (Cambridge, 1961), p. 229.

he may have been driven by a desire to mold a whole generation of worthwhile men to take the place of the son he could not have.

George Lewis and his wife were invited to Mount Vernon, the absences from his regiment during the war long since forgotten.

Bob Lewis, a member of the presidential household, went to church, made calls, took coach rides with his aunt, and wrote numerous letters for his uncle. The president was busy with "appointments, Customs, the Tr.," Bob recorded in his journal. Sunday was "generally a dull day with us," but the young man kept himself entertained. "[I am] happy to find myself so agreeable, indeed, uncommon facetious— being as it were, like a bird just escaped from captivity . . . I plunged [my] hand into a bosom to retrieve a wandering insect."

Bob also found time to have a locket made for his sister to hold locks of the hair of her deceased children. "I shall be extremely happy to make you a present of the same, as it may not only serve to bring to your remembrance the idea of the children you loved, but at the same time be a lasting memento of my love and attachment for your person." To his mother Bob confided, "I am, of so much more consequence here, than when at home, that I believe, I shall never be content to live any where else."

After Bob was married, however, he acted as business manager for his uncle in western Virginia. Washington chided his nephew for not collecting rents and not reporting land purchases. Once Bob "did well." And his uncle always sent "best wishes to Mrs. L." and signed letters with affection. Just before Christmas in 1792 Washington gave Bob a generous gift. "When you was at Mount Vernon you expressed a wish to be possessed of the stud horse that was there. If he is not sold . . . I make you a present of him." The next year a present of land was given, which had come to Washington from his mother. Unfortunately, title to it was not clear, and Washington was little help in solving the problem. Mary Ball Washington had been left the land by her father. "What his Christian name was I am not able to tell you; nor the county he lived in with certainty."

In October, 1795 Washington wrote Bob, "I am sorry you should have been so unsuccessful in purchasing in my life leases . . . there surely never was such a mistake as you have committed in this business, or I must have been out of my head when I wrote the letter." It was indeed a period of tremendous agitation for the aging president. He had caused his old friend (and nephews' law teacher) Secretary of State Edmund Randolph to resign because of suspected treason. Four men subsequently refused Washington's offer of Randolph's cabinet office.

When Bob Lewis left the presidential household in 1792, Washington wrote his sister that he wanted to hire her son Howell as a secretary. Howell was to reply in his own hand.

"I consider myself extremely favour'd by your proposal of a birth in your family and shall cheerfully accept it," Howell wrote his uncle in his best writing. "Howell my Dear Brother," wrote Betty, "is a Boy of very Slender Education His Fathers Death at so Early a Period has been a great disadvantage to him. However he has an exceeding Good disposition." In Tobias Lear's opinion, "Mr. Lewis possesses excellent dispositions; but unfortunately he has been too much in the habits of a young Virginian; but I trust a few years residence with the President will correct them." At the unexpected death of Mount Vernon manager Anthony Whiting however, Howell was dispatched to the plantation "to attend to executing of orders" until Washington could provide a new manager.

Washington would have preferred older nephew Lawrence Lewis to Howell as a secretary-aide ("on account of his age"), but had heard Lawrence was on the point of matrimony. He asked about him anyway. Was Lawrence "clear in his perceptions, and of good judgment . . . sober and sedate, or fond of amusements and running about? Was I at home myself, I should prefer a person connected with me as he is, to a more skilful man that was not (provided he had no thoughts of soon forming a matrimonial

alliance) because he could aid me in attentions to company." Three years before Lawrence had lost a young wife
in childbirth. Betty had written George about it. "I was on
a Visit to my Son Lawrence in Essex at the time I Expect'd
his wife to lyin. Pore thing it Proved fatal to her, she was
takein with Fitts and died in twelve Ours without being
Deliver'd, he lost a very good wife and with her all the Fortune as she was not of Age to make a Right to any part."

Lawrence did not marry again then; the rumors were
false. Several years later he would "form a matrimonial
alliance" of which his uncle would thoroughly approve.

While at Mount Vernon Howell Lewis received the same
long letters Washington always sent his managers. Because
of the yellow fever epidemic that summer which was killing
upwards of thirty-five hundred people Martha had stayed
into the fall at Mount Vernon. "As your Aunt may wish to
see my letters to you, always show them to her," Washington wrote Howell. Early in 1794 the new manager, William
Pearce, finally arrived and the letters to Howell ceased. "I
have sometimes thought him," Howell once wrote of his
uncle, "decidedly the handsomest man I ever saw; and when
in a lively mood, so full of pleasantry, so agreeable to all
with whom he was associated, that I could hardly realize
that he was the same Washington whose dignity awed all
who approached him."

Betty had a daughter—"a sprightly agreeable woman"
named Elizabeth, who had married Charles Carter and was
the recipient of some attention from her uncle. "Give my
love to Mrs. Carter and thank her for the letter she wrote
to me. . . . The remainder of the money due me for the
purchase of the lots . . . I give . . . to my niece, Mrs. Carter.
. . . Give my love to her," Washington instructed.

The letters between Washington and his sister Betty, in
the years immediately after their mother's death, show a
genuine fondness for one another. Except for alcoholic
Charles they were the only siblings left. "I am, my dear

sister, your most affectionate brother," Washington wrote. "My sincere Love and Best wishes attend you and my Sister Washington and Children," Betty replied.

At first Washington thought Betty would inherit one-fifth of their mother's property "not disposed of by the will." But because Mary had held the property under the will of her husband who had "made a distribution of it after her death," Betty was out of luck. She wrote George: "There are several articles in my possession which our mother left you. . . . They can be of little or no service to you, and of very great to me. I will thank you for them. If however you think them worth sending for, I have no wish to retain them."

Since her husband's death, Betty had tried to make ends meet by farming and by turning her home into a school. A 1794 letter from her succinctly expresses the southern economic dilemma concerning slavery. Betty asked her brother for advice on how to proceed with two Negroes who had run away to Philadelphia in hopes that they would be free there. "[They are] two of the Principal hands on the Pl . . . the hole Crop I made the last year was thirty Barrils of Corn and a Hundred and tenn Bushels of Wheat, if I am so unfortunate as not to git them again, I have no Chance to make anything the insuing year."

In 1783 Betty had asked George to have a chariot for four horses made for her in Philadelphia. Thirteen years later she would not be able to visit Mount Vernon for lack of transportation. She was down to "two old horses" when "my stable was broken open and the best carr'd off." It was "the forth charriot Hors that I lost in Fredericksburg you may Believe I had no great Parsiallity for the Place. Attacks of ague and fever which is attended with a cough" have laid her low. Nineteen days later Betty received George's "very affectionate letter. . . . My Dear Brother it is with Infinite Pleasure I here you intend to retire to your owne Home." Betty would no longer be in Fredericksburg. She planned to sell her house there, and move near her daughter in western Virginia. Her brother was persuaded she would have "fewer vexations, enjoy more ease and quiet. . . . It is my sincere wish that you should do so and that your days may be happy."

Shortly after his retirement from the presidency Betty died. The weary former president wrote her son George an unemotional letter, which expressed his usual philosophy toward death. "The melancholy of your writing has filled me with inexpressable concern. . . . The debt of nature however sooner or later, must be paid by us all, and although the separation from our nearest relatives is a heart rending circumstance, reason, religion and philosophy, teach us to bear it with resignation, while time alone can ameliorate, and soften the pangs we experience at parting.

"It must have been a consoling circumstances to my deceased Sister, that so many of her friends were about her," Washington added. Then curiously, he went on in the next sentence to talk about the work being done on Mount Vernon. There is not another reference to Betty in his *Writings*.

No correspondence with brother Charles during the presidential years survives. Harriot claimed that he was in good health in 1794. Was Harriot unobservant or tactful? Eight years earlier Washington had written of Charles's attachment to the bottle.

Charles had two daughters, Frances and Mildred, with whom Washington seems to have been on good terms. "I . . . congratulate you on the birth of a Son," he wrote Frances's husband, Burgess Ball, and the passage of your family through the Small Pox." A box was sent "containing bracelets, &ca for Mrs. Ball." "I am glad to find by your letter that the bracelets were received, and pleased," Washington wrote a few weeks later. "Milly" thanked her uncle for a cloak he had sent her.

When Charles's son Samuel (George Augustine's younger brother) married, he had been given the management of his father's property and debts (as well as of his Uncle

Sam's). The young man had a rough time of it, in spite of the usual advice from Uncle George. "There is no person fonder of receiving Advice than what I am," Samuel assured him. It was just as well.

"Love Is A Mighty Pretty Thing"

*A*lthough only a relative by marriage, daughter-in-law Nelly's second husband, David Stuart, was a confidant of Washington's as his own brothers had been years before. Stuart was one of three men appointed by the president as commissioners to the new district of Columbia. July 26, 1789, George Washington to David Stuart: "In the first moment of my ability to sit in an easy chair, and that not entirely without pain, I occupy myself in acknowledging the receipt, and thanking you for your letter . . . your communications, without any reserve will be exceedingly grateful and pleasing to me. . . . I should like to be informed . . . not so much what may be thought commendable parts, if any, of my conduct, as of those which are conceived to be of a different complexion."

Dr. Stuart had written that there was "clamor and abuse" against Vice-President Adams for the number of horses had for his carriage. Patrick Henry said "it squinted towards monarchy." Washington's conduct on the other hand "was spoke of, with high approbation and particularly your dispensing with ceremony occasionally, and walking the streets."

To Stuart the president complained about the Senate. "Why they keep their doors shut, when acting in a Legislative capacity, I am unable to inform you; unless it is because they think there is too much speaking to the Gallery in the other House, and business is thereby retarded."

And of the press. "It is to be lamented that the Editors of the different Gazettes in the Union do not more generally, and more correctly (instead of stuffing their papers with scurrility, and nonsensical declamation, which few would read if they were apprised of the contents) publish the debates in Congress on all great national questions. . . ." To Stuart he revealed opinions, confided decisions. "Your description of the public mind in Virginia, gives me pain. It seems to be more irritable, sour, and discontented than . . . in any other State in the Union, except Massachusetts.

"As none but the officers of Govt. have been made acquainted with my determination respecting the ratif. of the [Jay] T[reaty] (as communicated to you last night) I request you would say nothing concerning it yourself to others."

Betsey Custis considered her stepfather, David Stuart, a "gloomy mortal" and never forgave him for moving her and her sister from Abingdon to Hope Park. Not recorded are her mother Nelly's feelings about the fact that by Jacky Custis and David Stuart she gave birth at least twenty times. Tobias Lear had something to say about it. "Mr. Stuart goes on in the usual way producing a new inhabitant to the United States every year."

Glimpses of the older Custis girls who with their mother remained close to the Washingtons are seen in family letters. When Betsey was born, Jacky had written his mother: "I cannot pretend to say who the baby is like. It is as much like Dr. Rumney as anybody else, she has a double chin or something like it, in point of fatness, with fine black hair and eyes. Upon the whole, I think it is as fine a baby as ever

I saw. This is not my opinion alone, but the opinion of all who have seen her."

Her father had been "the handsomest youth of his day . . . soon fell desperately in love with my mother," Betsey wrote a friend in 1808. Aunt Patsy "adored her brother."

As a young child, "I had a good memory and learned many songs . . . my father and Dr. R. taught me many very improper ones, and I can now remember standing on the table when not more than 3 or 4 years old, singing songs which I did not understand—while my father and other gentlemen were often rolling in their chairs with laughter . . . my mother remonstrated in vain . . . and her husband always said his little Bet could not be injured by what she did not understand—that he had no boy and she must make fun for him, untill he did." (One of Washington's biographers points to this scene as evidence of Jacky Custis's "sinister"[25] behavior. He makes no criticism of Eleanor Custis, who according to Betsey "could not help laughing.")

Once Betsey's father punished her for putting cottonseed up her nose. "My proud heart swelled with anger. [I] did not mind pain. . . . [He] disgraced me before other children. . . . It was "hard they would not teach me Greek and Latin because I was a girl." Instead, she was instructed in "mending, writing, arithmetic, and music." Her father feared Betsey "would be miserable" as she grew older—a "prophetic" observation.

Wash was "the darling of my grandmother, always in her arms." Betsey loved her grandmother "more than my mother . . . my heart always broke, when she was obliged to go to the Genrl." When the sisters rejoined their grandparents at Mount Vernon, "Patty and I were half crazy for joy. It was our greatest pleasure to go to Mount Vernon."

Betsey was "frantic" when Washington left. The election of her grandfather caused "serious injury to my health." For twenty-one days she had "a nervous fever." Patty was

25. Flexner, *George Washington* II, p. 446n.

"of a different turn" from her sister. "She was the favorite of my mother's family—of whom I was less fond." The two sisters were "constantly together, yet never alike."

Betsey was not always petulant and neurotic. John Adams reported favorably on her to Abigail. "One of them is a fine, blooming rosy girl, who I dare say has more liberty than Nelly."[26] Abigail Adams herself found Betsey "a very pleasing, agreeable Lady . . . easy, tranquil, unaffected [who] seems to inherit all the benevolence of her Grandmother."[27]

When sister Patty was married to Thomas Peter of Georgetown, Betsey did show unmistakable signs of jealousy. Perhaps in an attempt to feel loved, she asked her grandfather for his picture. His reply—written just as he was about to depart for the "whiskey campaign"—was affectionate and sensitive. "My dear Betcy: Shall I, in answer to your letter . . . say, when you are as near the *Pinnacle* of happiness as your sister Patcy conceives herself ₔo be; or when your candour shines more conspicuously than it does in *that* letter, that I will *then,* comply with the request you have made, for my Picture?

"No: I will grant it without either. . . . Respect may place it among the desirable objects of it [your heart], but there are emotions of a softer kind, to wch. the heart of a girl turned eighteen, is susceptible, that must have generated much warmer ideas, although the fruition of them may be more distant than those of your Sister's." This was followed by a thoughtful description of the basis for a good marriage.

A year-and-a-half later after "a lucky escape" from another suitor according to Nelly, Betsey had a man of her own—Thomas Law, "an English gentleman, but last from the East-Indies, of considerable fortune," who was speculating on land development in the federal city. Betsey was

26. John Adams, *Letters of John Adams Addressed to His Wife II* (Boston, 1841), p. 176.

27. Abigail Adams, *New Letters of Abigail Adams* (Boston, 1947), pp. 34, 140.

nineteen; Law was thirty-nine and had three sons. February 7, 1796, George Washington to David Stuart: "I find . . . that Betsey Custis has cast her lot; very much to her own satisfaction, having given it due weight and consideration in *every* point of view she could place the matter: of course disparity in age could not have escaped. Mr. Law, so far as I have obtained any knowledge of his character, is a respectable man and much esteemed; and may, at least in a degree, be an agent; for which reasons, I think prudence requires, and as a man of honor he cannot refuse, to make a settlement upon her previous to marriage; of her own fortune if [sic] no more."

Three days later Washington wrote Betsey in the joshing yet serious tone he reserved for his granddaughters. "My dear Betsey: I have obeyed your injunction in not acknowledging the receipt of your letter . . . until I should hear from Mr. Law. This happened yesterday; I therefore proceed to assure you, if Mr. Law is the man of your choice . . . that your alliance with him meets my approbation. *Yes,* Betsey, and this approbation is accompanied in this important event as your most Sanguine imagination has ever presented to your view. . . . You know how much I love you, how much I have been gratified by your attentions to those things which you had reason to believe were grateful to my feelings. And having *no* doubt of your continuing the *same* conduct . . . I shall remain with the sincerest friendship, and the most Affectionate regard, etc."

The relations between Thomas Law and Washington were apparently cordial. "It gives us much pleasure to hear that Mrs. Law, yourself and the child were all well, and that the latter begins, so soon, to learn the use of her feet," the president wrote him a few years later. Law *was* irritable. "Mr. Law is waiting, and you know he does not wait patiently for anything not even for dinner," Washington concluded a letter to a mutual friend.

Of Patty Custis her grandmother wrote, "I really believe she is a very deserving girl." Tobias Lear's opinion was that

"Patsy is said to bid fair to make the finest woman of the three."

Patty's husband, Thomas Peter, was "the best and most affectionate," wrote sister Nelly. Their little girl was "a very fat, handsome, good tempered, clever toad" named Martha Eliza Eleanor Peter, "a way of getting quit of all the family names at once." A year later she "walks very well, will soon talk, has many teeth and is the fattest, most saucy, charming, entertaining little monkey," according to doting Aunt Nelly. A number of brothers and sisters followed, two born before their great-grandfather died. There was frequent contact with Mount Vernon. "Mrs. Peter and the Child are well. . . . Mr., Mrs. and Eleanor Peter are well at this place. . . . Mrs. Peter has got another daughter," Washington wrote. "I congratulate you and Patcy on the birth of a 'Manchild'," he wrote Thomas Peter. "My best wishes attend the Mother and Child."

A request from Thomas for a loan to purchase land in the new federal city was turned down, but that was not unusual. As Washington once wrote a nephew who requested a second loan four months after a first, "I perceive by your letter . . . that you are under the same mistake that many others are in supposing that I have money always at Command."

George Washington had always been cash poor, in spite of surveying jobs, military service, and Martha's dowry. (The children's and grandchildren's part of the Custis inheritance was always applied strictly to their needs.) Mount Vernon barely sustained itself, wartime inflation drastically depreciated bonds Washington had invested in, and the collection of rents from tenants on lands in western Virginia was never very effective. During the war General Washington received no salary; payment for his expenses was undoubtedly as erratic and undependable as supplies for the troops. Congress provided a generous salary of twenty-five thousand dollars a year for the presidency. (Secretary Lear's, in comparison, was five hundred dollars.) Washington refused the salary, but collected for presidential expenses, which came to the same amount. It is difficult to determine how any cash was available to supplement brother Sam's meager estate for his children or for George to buy an affectionate present for one of his intimate relations.

"I Close My Public Life"

I close my public life the 4th of March," Washington wrote nephew Bob Lewis early in 1797, "after which no consideration under heaven that I can foresee shall again with draw me from the walks of private life."

The president's "Farewell Address" had been printed and distributed the previous fall. Bart Dandridge reported that he had been unable to discover "a single instance of disapprobation of any part thereof."[28] This may have alleviated the hurt both Washington and his wife felt over bitter criticisms in the Republican press of their life-style, their friendship with conservatives. Tobias Lear who mixed "with people in different walks, high and low, of different descriptions and of different political sentiments," had tried to convince the couple that many of the attacks were in

28. Flexner, *George Washington* IV, p. 304.

effect Federalist "dirty tricks" to turn the president against the Republicans.

During the last months in office Washington had an uncomfortable set of false teeth replaced, went to the theater and a concert, gave a prodigious number of parties. "Large company of the Honorable Congress to dine. They like to hear musick although they do not know one note from another," wrote irrepressible Nelly Custis. "All the Diplomatic Corps (except France) dined with me," Washington recorded in his diary. French Minister Adet had given to both the secretary of state and the hateful *Aurora* a copy of the Directory's response to the Jay treaty with Great Britain—a resolution that all neutrals would be treated the same as England. This effectively put an end to American trade with West Indian ports. The secretary of state's reply was greeted with an inflammatory phamphlet circulated by Adet. In addition, by late February there were rumors that France had not recognized the new ambassador sent by the United States to France.

Twelve thousand people crowded into Rickett's amphitheater to pay homage to the retiring president at a ball on his sixty-sixth birthday. They were "in danger of being squeezed to death." But the occasion was a momentous one for the elderly couple. Martha was "moved even to tears"[29] by the adulation. Washington's "emotions were too powerful to be concealed. He could sometimes scarcely speak."[30]

At the March, 1797 inauguration of John Adams as president and Thomas Jefferson as vice-president, George Washington still held the limelight, in spite of his genuine efforts to shift public attention to the new executive. Nelly was "terribly agitated,"[31] a spectator observed.

During the next few days farewells were made and presents exchanged. Tobias Lear had arrived and would stay behind to tend to final business. Bart Dandridge was to

29. Ibid., p. 332.
30. Ibid.
31. Charles Moore, *The Family Life of George Washington* (Boston & New York, 1926), p. 143.

depart for The Hague. Ninety-seven boxes, fourteen trunks, forty-three casks, thirteen packages, and three hampers were packed for the trip to Mount Vernon. All the way home "inhabitants were out to see and be seen and welcome . . . my dear Grandpapa," wrote Nelly. A letter from George Washington to Lear included a good-natured P.S. "On the one side, I am called upon to remember the parrot; on the other, to remember the dog. For my own part, I should not pine much if both were forgot." At the federal city the family "Dined at Mr. Law's and lodged at Mr. Thos. Peters."

Living at Mount Vernon was "a dream," wrote Nelly to a friend. "I can hardly realize my being here. Grandpapa is very well, and much pleased with being once more *Farmer Washington.*" To Wash at school in New Jersey "Farmer Washington" wrote, "We are all in a litter and dirt occasioned by joiners, masons, and painters working in the house." His grandfather "approve[s] your determination to come directly to Mount Vernon." It was a time for all the immediate family to be home together.

V

RETIREMENT

1797–1799

"A Strong Interest in Your Welfare"

*I*t was that immediate family which now shared with his plantation George Washington's full attention. His letters concerning troublesome grandson George Washington Parke Custis (just before and after retirement) bear an uncanny resemblance to those about Wash's father, Jacky, written years before. After an unsuccessful learning experience in Philadelphia and a few months dithering in Virginia, Wash had been sent to the college at Princeton, New Jersey. (There was no longer a Jonathan Boucher railing against it.)

November 15, 1796, George Washington to G. W. P. Custis: "Yesterday's mail brought me your letter . . . and under cover of this letter you will receive a ten-dollar bill, to purchase a gown, &c., if proper. . . . It affords me pleasure to hear that you are agreeably fixed; and I receive still more from the assurance you give of attending closely to your studies. . . . Endeavor to conciliate the good will of *all* your fellow-students, rendering them every act of kindness in your power. Be particularly obliging and attentive to your chamber-mate. . . . One thing more and I will close this letter. Never let an indigent person ask, without receiving *something,* if you have the means; always recollecting in what light the widow's mite was viewed. . . ."

November 16, 1796, George Washington to Tobias Lear: "Washington Custis has got settled at Princeton College, and I think under favorable auspices, but the change from his former habits is so great and sudden; and his hours for study so much increased beyond what he has been accustomed to, that though he promises to be attentive, it is easy to be perceived he is not at all reconciled to it yet."

November 28, 1796, George Washingto to G. W. P. Custis: "The assurances you give me of applying diligently to your studies . . . are highly pleasing and satisfactory to me. . . . P. S. I presume you have received my letter covering a ten-dollar bill to pay for your gown, although it is not mentioned."

December 19, 1796, George Washington to G. W. P. Custis: ". . . we are always glad to hear from you, though we do not wish that letter writing should interfere with your more useful and profitable occupation. . . . The pleasure of hearing you were well, in good spirits, and progressing as we could wish in your studies, was communicated . . . to your grandmama; but what gave me particular satisfaction, was to find that you were going to commence a course of reading with Doctor Smith, of such books as he had chosen for that purpose. . . . Adieu, I sincerely wish you well, being your attached and affectionate friend."

Washington had needed something to give him "particular satisfaction" that last fall of the presidency when the French were acting up. In addition, old Revolutionary War supporter Thomas Paine had published *Letter to Washington,* a cruel and insulting pamphlet.

February 27, 1797, George Washington to G. W. P. Custis: Washington is gratified that Wash is "attentive to and pleased by your studies." But is membership in the Whig

Society sanctioned by his professors? And a timeless assurance: "your Grand Mamma will be attentive to the articles you left here."

March 25, 1797, G. W. P. Custis to George Washington: "I think I have spent my time in a manner not to be complained of." Wash is "perfect" in Roman history, quite familiar with French, his writing has improved, and he has read "a great many authors. . . . I must confess not much progress in arithmetic."

April 3, 1797, George Washington to G. W. P. Custis: Grandpapa is still pleased with the scholar—an improvement in his writing is visible, "both in characters and diction."

So far, so good. But after the vacation at Mount Vernon during May, Wash sent a letter from Princeton which broached the possibility of giving up his studies—with predictable results. Washington replied firmly in the negative, than waited anxiously for a response. May 29, 1797, G. W. P. Custis to George Washington: "Good God, how just your letter!" Wash's soul has been "tortured with stings of conscience." Now he has "a heart overflowing with joy at the success of conscience over disposition. . . . I will now make a grand exertion, and show you that your grandson shall once more deserve your favor."

June 4, 1797, George Washington to G. W. P. Custis: "Your letter . . . eased my mind . . . your resolution to abandon ideas expressed." Only Wash's grandmama and sister know of his momentary lapse of scholarly resolve.

June 8, 1797, G. W. P. Custis to George Washington: Wash's heart is still "overflowing with joy" as well as "gratitude and love." Washington's letter is "engraven on my mind."

But Grandpapa was concerned over Wash's courses. "I do not hear you mention anything of geography or mathematics." Wash hurried to reassure him. He was "now engaged in geography" and English grammar too. In August another nudge went out from Mount Vernon. "The senior class having left . . . ought to provoke strong stimu-

lus to those who remain, to acquire equal reputation.
Washington enclosed money for the vacation journey home.
"Both your grandmama and myself desire" that Wash not
travel by water (because of accidents) or by Philadelphia
(because of yellow fever).

During the vacation home Wash announced that he did
not wish to return to Princeton. His grandfather remonstrated. But that fall a regretful letter was sent from George
Washington to the Reverend Smith, president of Princeton, October 9, 1797: "I have duly received your several
letters of last month; but as an expression of my regret, at
the conduct and behavior of young Custis would avail
nothing I shall not trouble you by the attempt.

"I am persuaded that your conduct towards him, has been
such as friendship inspired, and the duties of your important trust required. And as you have seen, in a degree what
my solicitude, advice and admonition have been, he will
have himself only to unbraid for any consequences which
may follow, and this perhaps come too late."

After an unproductive fall at Mount Vernon, sixteen-
year-old Wash was given a set of rules by his grandfather:

"System in all things should be aimed at; for in execu-
tion, it renders every thing more easy.

"If now and then of a morning before breakfast, you are
inclined, by way of change, to go out with a Gun, I shall
not object to it; provided you return by the hour we usually
set down to that meal.

"From breakfast, until about an hour before Dinner
(allowed for dressing, and preparing for it, that you may
appear decent) I shall expect you will confine yourself to
your studies; and diligently attend to them; endeavouring
to make yourself master of whatever is recommended to,
or required of you.

"While the afternoons are short, and but little interval
between rising from dinner and assembling for Tea, you
may employ that time in walking, or any other recreation.

"After Tea, if the studies you are engaged in require it,
you will, no doubt perceive the propriety and advantage of
returning to them, until the hour of rest.

"Rise early, that by habit it may become familiar, agreeable, healthy, and profitable. It may for a while, be irksome to do this, but that will wear off; and the practise will produce a rich harvest forever thereafter; whether in public, or private walks of life.

"Make it an invariable rule to be in place (unless extraordinary circumstances prevent it) at the usual breakfasting, dining, and tea hours. It is not only disagreeable, but it is also very inconvenient, for servants to be running here, and ther, and they know not where, to summon you to them, when their duties, and attendance on the company who are seated, render it improper.

"Saturday may be appropriated to riding; to your Gun, and other proper amusements.

"Time disposed of in this manner, makes ample provision for exercise and every useful, or necessary recreation; at the same time that the hours allotted for study, *if really applied to it* instead of running up and down stairs, you wasted in conversation with any one who will talk with you, will enable you to make considerable progress in whatever line is marked out for you, and that you may do it, is my sincere wish."

In later years Washington Custis remembered that his grandfather shed tears when reprimanding him for "manifold errors and follies." Long letters to David Stuart written in January and February, 1798 show they were tears of frustration and love. "What is best done with him, I know not. . . . I am perfectly satisfied from the experience of the last few months that he has been here, that even under the constant care of a more illumined Preceptor than I am sure there is the least chance of obtaining, he would progress very little; as as the case now is, that he will forget what he does know, so inert is his mind."

On March 5, 1798, "Doctr. Stuart left this to accompany Washington Custis to St. John's College at Annapolis," Washington wrote in his diary. The same day he wrote Mr. McDowell, the head of the college. "Mr. Custis possesses competetent talents to fit him for any studies, but they are counteracted by an indolence of mind which renders it difficult to draw them into action . . . justice from me, requires I should add, that I know of no Vice to which this inertness can be attributed. From drinking and gaming he is perfectly free, and if he has a propensity to any other impropriety, it is hidden from me. He is generous, and regardful of truth."

The letters between Wash and his grandfather in the subsequent months sound like those to and from Princeton. Wash "constantly bear[s] in mind your virtuous precepts." Grandpapa receives "much pleasure to find that you are agreeably fixed, disposed to prosecute your studies with zeal and alacrity."

The pleasure was short-lived. In May Wash asked, "To whom am I to apply for money in case of need?" From Mount Vernon came an anguished reply. "I am at a loss to discover what has given rise to so early a question." In June Wash fell in love. "I have said that none of us have heard from you," wrote his grandfather, "but it behooves me to add, that from persons in Alexandria, lately from Annapolis, I have, with much surprise, been informed of your devoting much time, and paying much attention, to a certain young lady of that place. . . . I am sure this is not a time for a *boy of your age* to enter into engagements which might end in sorrow and repentance."

Wash was quick to defend himself. "The report as mamma tells me, of my being *engaged* to the young lady in question, is strictly erroneous. That I gave her reason to believe in my attachment to her, I candidly allow, but that I would *enter into engagements* inconsistent with my duty or situation, I hope your good opinion of me will make you disbelieve."

"My brother will be home in August," Nelly wrote a friend. "He is much pleased with Annapolis and studies well." Wash had now finished Euclid, he wrote his grandfather, "and with that, the course marked out for me while in Annapolis." He was sending home his accounts. Is he "to leave entirely, or not, so that I May pack accordingly."

"Washn. Custis came home frm. College," noted Washington abruptly in his diary August 15. It was a wild time to be at Mount Vernon. "Farmer Washington" was engaged in a power struggle with his successor, President Adams. Angered by French attacks on American shipping and the insulting, insidious XYZ affair, Washington supported Adams's intention to prepare for war. He abandoned his vow to remain a private citizen and accepted the president's appointment as commander of an army to be raised if fighting was necessary. But Washington insisted ("hysterically,"[32] says biographer Flexner) on choosing the other generals and threatened to resign when Adams crossed him. The former president's disposition was not helped by, nor did it help, the moody adolescent in his household. To David Stuart Washington sent a plea for help. "If you, or Mrs. Stuart could, by indirect means, discover the State of Washington Custis's mind, it would be to be wished. He appears to be moped and Stupid says nothing, and is always in some hole or corner excluded from Company. Before he left Annapolis, he wrote to me desiring to know whether he was to return there, or not, that he might pack up accordingly; I answered, that I was astonished at the question! and that it appeared to me that nothing that could be said to him had the least effect, or left an impression beyond the moment. Whether this, by thwarting his views, is the cause of his present behaviour, I know not."

In September Washington made one more attempt to persuade Wash to return to college. It was no use. "Although he professed his readiness to do whatever was required of him," Washington wrote President McDowell, "his unwillingness to return was too apparent to afford any hope that good would result from it in the prosecution of his studies." Mr. Lear "who I have taken as my Military Secretary" was asked to attend to Wash's reading as well.

At President Adams's request the old warrior was back in Philadelphia in November, "making a selection of Offi-

32. Flexner, *George Washington IV*, p. 412.

cers for the twelve new Regiments, and arranging them to the different States." Two lengthy letter-reports to the secretary of war written on December 13 indicate that Washington had risen to the challenge with zest. A private letter written to the secretary the next day is an echo of one Washington wrote years before to Jonathan Boucher about Jacky Custis's proposed European trip. Washington Custis had been nominated "as a Cornet in the Troop proposed to be commanded by my nephew Lawrence Lewis . . . Having requested that the Nomination of Mr. Custis might be with held . . . until I could consult his Grandmother (Mrs. Washington) and Mother (Mrs. Stuart), I further pray that no mention of his name for such an Office may be made, until that matter is ascertained; because if their consent being an only son, indeed the only Male of his family, cannot be had, it would be better that the arrangement of him should pass *entirely* unnoticed to prevent the uneasy sensations wch. might otherwise arise in his breast."

Martha "does not seem to have the least objection to his acceptance of the Commission," it turned out, and neither did Nelly Custis Stuart. January 10, 1799 the secretary of war appointed Wash a Cornet. He became aide de camp to General Pinckney and was soon promoted to colonel. The French threat simmered down, however, and by fall both Wash's and Lawrence Lewis's brief military careers were over. The problem of what to do about Washington's beloved grandson was not.

"Every Blessing Is Bestowed On You"

$\mathcal{G}$randmama always spoils Washington," Nelly Custis once complained. But by the time she was eighteen and Wash was sixteen, Nelly thought her "dearest Brother" was "very much grown and astonishingly improved." Nelly herself—the little "wild creature," the "half-crazy" teen-aged girl described by her grandmother years before—had been replaced by a self-assured young woman.

Visitors to Mount Vernon were entranced. According to architect Benjamin Latrobe, she had "more perfection of form, of expression, of color, of softness, and of firmness of mind than I have ever seen before or conceived consistent with mortality. She is everything that the chisel of Phidias aimed at but could not reach, and the soul beaming through the countenance and glowing in her smile is as superior to her face as mind is to matter."

"She appeared modest, well-bred, intelligent, and sensible, has a piercing eye, grecian nose, made judicious remarks and conversed with propriety," reported a more restrained observer." Polish nobleman Niemcewicz was as smitten as Latrobe. "She was one of those celestial beings so rarely produced by nature, sometimes dreamed of by poets and painters, which one cannot see without a feeling of ectasy. Her sweetness equals her beauty, and that is perfect. She has many accomplishments. She plays the piano, she sings, and designs better than the usual woman of America, or even of Europe."

Fortunately, the personality of this paragon emerges from her letters. Writing to Philadelphia friend Elizabeth Borddley, she speaks affectionately of Patty's family. "I am in Sister Peter's room, Patty and child asleep, Thomas reading. . . . I am housekeeper nurse." Sister Betsey was engaged; Nelly guessed that she and Elizabeth would be spinsters. She wished to be called Eleanor from then on as "Nelly is extremely homely." She had been to a few "sober, small tea parties," but dancing was Nelly's delight. She "care[d] not a fig" for the races, but danced at a Birth Night ball in Alexandria until 2 A.M., stayed up until 5. One partner had "a pug nose and ugly mouth," another was "a fop . . . ressembled a Spaniel," Nelly wrote breezily. Young Mr. Carroll with whom she danced six times was "very tall, well made, fair with blue eyes and fine light hair." But he had been "too often told of his merit [which] has given him more affectation than agreeable."

When Nelly was a bridesmaid at sister Betsey's wedding, she wrote her grandparents an unenthusiastic description of a Georgetown ball. It prompted a wise and delightful reply from her grandfather. (Martha's comments about the ball were shorter but just as perceptive: "[One] always expects more pleasure than they realize after the matter is over.") Nelly wrote "a fair hand" and "[your] ideas are lively and your descriptions agreeable," Grandpapa told her. She should begin a new paragraph when changing the subject. "—Let me touch a little now on your Georgetown ball; and happy, thrice happy, for the fair who were assembled on the occasion, that there was a man to spare;—for had there been 79 ladies and only 78 gentlemen, there might, in the course of the evening, have been some disorder among the caps;—notwithstanding the apathy which *one* of the company entertain for the youth of the present day, and her determination '*never* to give herself a moments uneasiness on account of any of them.' A hint here;—Men and women feel the same inclinations toward each other *now* that they always have done, and which they will continue to do until there is a new order of things, and *you,* as others have done, may find, perhaps, that the passions of your sex are easier raised than allayed. Do not therefore boast too soon or too strongly of your insensibility to, or resistance of its powers."

Grandpapa had some practical advice. "When the fire is beginning to kindle, and your heart growing warm, propound these questions to it. Who is this invader? Have I competent knowledge of him? Is he a man of good character, a man of sense? . . . What has been his walk in life? Is he a gambler, a spendthrift, or a drunkard? Is his fortune sufficient to maintain me in the manner I have been accustomed to live, and my sisters do live, and is he one to whom my friends can have no reasonable objection? Grandpapa closed with a benediction: . . . every blessing, among which a good husband when you want and deserve one, is bestowed on you."

An impression was made. Nelly wrote Elizabeth: "My husband I must first love him with all my Heart—that is not Romantically, but [with] esteem . . . that man [I am] not yet acquainted with." It was decidedly not Mr. Carroll. "[I am] not now, nor [have] been engaged to C.C.," Nelly wrote heatedly after a letter from her brother hinted as much.

Although Grandpapa discouraged political conversations at mealtime, Nelly was "becoming an outrageous politician, perfectly federal." If drowning, she would "trust a straw sooner than the stability of the French republican government [and its] barbarous democratic murders."

Nelly's ardor was increased by her close friendship with

George Washington Motier Lafayette, son of the general, who was sent to President Washington by his mother after the family had been held prisoner in Austria as a result of the French Revolution. (Lafayette, Sr., was still a captive.) The arrival of the fifteen-year-old boy and his tutor in Boston in the fall of 1795 had put the beleagured president in a quandary. "My dear Young friend," he wrote George Lafayette. "It was with sincere pleasure I received your letter from Boston, and with the heart of affection I welcome you to this Ctry." But "considerations of a political nature" made it a matter of propriety for George to remain incognito in Boston for the time being. The president would pay George's expenses, but dared not invite him into his home.

A pair of agonized letters went to Secretary Hamilton. "On one side, I may be charged with countenancing those who have been denouncing the enemies of France; on the other with *not* countenancing the Son of a man who is dear to America." "His case gives me pain, and I do not know how to get relieved from it. His sensibility I fear is hurt, by his not acknowledging the receipt of my letter to him."

By February, 1796 Washington dared suggest to George and his companion a spring visit to Mount Vernon. "By that time the weather will be settled, the roads good, and the travelling pleasant." Besides, pro–French revolutionary, anti-Federalists in Congress had allowed their humanitarian instincts to overcome their political ones, and supported a move to investigate a rumor that young Lafayette was in America and to see if he needed support.

"Young Fayette and his friend are with me," Washington wrote with satisfaction April 11 from Mount Vernon. That was the same spring Thomas Law was courting Betsey, Andrew Parks was courting Harriot, Martha was mourning Fanny's death, and Congress and the country were angrily debating the Jay treaty.

Nelly Custis was visisting her mother at Hope Park, but sped to Mount Vernon to join her grandparents and meet their French ward. "If Miss Nelly Custis should apply to you for a Cart to Transport her Trunk and other things from Doctor Stuarts to Mount Vernon, let it be done as soon as applied for," Washington eagerly instructed his Mount Vernon manager.

George Lafayette was "a gentle, melancholy, interesting youth," according to one visistor. In August Washington asked the postmaster general to alert postmasters in all coastal towns to forward letters addressed to George to Mount Vernon "as his anxiety to hear from, or of his Parents, can only be exceeded by his uneasiness at their unhappy situation." When Benjamin Latrobe visisted Mount Vernon that summer of 1796, he wrote observant comments about others there besides the radiant Nelly. George Lafayette had "a mild, pleasant countenance; his figure was awkward but manners easy with little of the usual French air." He had "wit and fluency . . . talked much with Nelly Custis." The family treated young Lafayette "more as a child than a guest."[33]

George returned to Philadelphia with the Washingtons in the fall. He was part of the retirement caravan the following March. But he left with his tutor in a hurry for New York and a transatlantic ship in October, on hearing a rumor that his father was free and back with his family in France. Washington was fearful for the young man, but not so much so that he could not take practical advantage of George's journey to convey the balance of Wash's tuition to Princeton.

George mailed an affectionate letter from New York to Nelly, "my dear sister, my good, my excellent friend." He had been "in your house as happy as I could be separated from my family." Mrs. Washington had been "a second mother." George carried an admiring letter from Washington to his father, a letter in sharp contrast to the ones about Wash. George's "conduct . . . has been exemplary in every point of view, such as has gained him the esteem, affection and confidence of all who have had the pleasure of his acquaintance." Washington was touched by George's

33. Ibid., p. 350.

"ardent desire to embrace his parents and Sisters in the first moments of their releasement." His companion too was praised. "No parent could have been more attentive to a favourite Son."

Months later came word that after "a long and disagreeable passage" George and his tutor were in England. They could not go ashore at France . . . but "our hopes are realized." All the family was safe at Hamburg on Danish territory. George sent to Mount Vernon his "gratitude and thanks." Washington penned a warm, newsy letter about family members to George on Christmas Day, 1798. "Mrs. Washington holds you in constant remembrance. When the clouds which at present overcast the Political horrison are dispelled, it would give all your friends great pleasure to see you in your old walks, and to none more than to your Sincere and affectionate friend."*

Washington's news to George about Nelly Custis was momentous. The previous fall after Washington had been retired for eight months Nelly described for her friend Elizabeth a romp with her brother. She "rode Sir. Ed. Pellew" to Alexandria and got drenched. Her hair was "like rats tails . . . beaver hat and feather completely soaked." For five days afterwards she had suffered a toothache and her face swelled. There was a casual afterthought. "We expect Mr. Lewis, a nephew of the President's to spend the winter here."

Widowed Mr. Lewis was the same Lawrence Lewis whom Washington had wanted to engage several years before, if he had no thoughts of a matrimonial alliance. "As both your aunt and I are in the decline of life, and regular in our habits, especially in our hours of rising and going to bed," his uncle wrote Lawrence soon after retirement, "I require some person (fit and Proper) to ease me of the trouble of entertaining company, particularly of nights as it is my

---

* Years later Nelly had the pleasure of welcoming George Lafayette and his elderly father to her home during their celebrated trip back to America.

inclination to retire . . . either to bed, or to my study, soon after candle-light."

In a subsequent letter to a friend Nelly painted a contented picture of life at Mount Vernon at that time. "We have spent our summer and autumn very happily here, having been in general blessed with good health, have had many agreeable visitors, and are now contentedly seated around our winter fireside, often speaking of and wishing to see again our good friends in Philadelphia, but never regretting its amusements, or a life of ceremony. I stay very much at home, have not been to the city for two or three months. I have never a dull or lonesome hour, never find a day too long, indeed the time seems to fly, and I sometimes think the years are shorter for some time past than they ever were."

The president's nephew may have had something to do with Nelly's outlook. It took her about a year to decide that Lawrence was the one she "must first love . . . with all my Heart" and for Lawrence to join the throng of Nelly Custis admirers. "Cupid, a small mischievous urchin . . . took me by surprise. . . [the] very moment that I had resolved [to] pass through life as a prim starched Spinster," Nelly wrote Elizabeth. "He slyly called in Lawrence Lewis to his aid and transfixed me with a Dart." Washington was even more surprised and equally coy. "Your acquaintance Lawrence Lewis is appointed Captain of a Troop of Light Dragoons," he wrote George Lafayette, "but intends, before he enters the Camp of Mars to engage in that of Venus; Eleanor Custis and he having entered into a contract of marriage; which I understand is to be fulfilled on my birthday."

The engagement had taken place while Washington was in Philadelphia organizing the army. Shortly after departing he had sent a letter to Lawrence with a laborious explanation of why he had made "enquiry into cause of my not seeing you the morning I left Mount Vernon. . . . It was not from a supposed disrespect on your part." Washington's mind was muddled and he couldn't remember whether he had seen Lawrence or not—which may account for his obtuseness in regard to the romance developing under his nose. "They having, while I was at Philadelphia, without my having the smallest suspicion that such an affair was in agitation, formed their Contract for this purpose," Washington happily wrote Bart Dandridge.

It was first necessary for Washington to sign papers in Alexandria making him Nelly's legal guardian "thereby to authorize a license for your nuptials." Close relatives were invited to the wedding. A special invitation went from Washington to touchy Thomas Law "lest Mrs. Law and yourself should require something more formal than an Invitation from the Bride Elect."[34]

The Stuarts, Peters, and Laws arrived February 11 and Lawrence's brother Bob Lewis soon afterward. February 22: "The Revd. Mr. Davis and Mr. Geo. Calvert came to dinner and Miss Custis was married abt. candle light to Mr. Lawe. Lewis," Washington recorded in his diary.

His pleasure over the event is better seen in a letter to Lawrence the following fall. The newlyweds had spent the summer visiting relatives all over Virginia and trying various health resorts and remedies in an attempt to cure Lawrence's eye inflammation. Lawrence had resigned his commission when relations with France improved. He expected to live with his bride at his house in Frederick County, Virginia. But Nelly had no intention of dwelling in a remote area, as her sisters and mother had had to do. September 20, 1799, George Washington to Lawrence Lewis: ". . . it has been understood from expressions occasionally dropped (from Nelly Custis, now) your Wife, that it is the wish of you both to settle in this neighborhood. . . . I shall inform you . . . that in the Will which I have by me . . . that part of my Mount Vernon tract which lies [on Dogue Run] is bequeathed to you and her jointly, if you incline to build on it; and few better sites for a house than Gray's hill, and that range are to be found in this County or elsewhere."

34. Original letter owned by Mrs. L. Johnson.

Nelly was "a sedate matron," she wrote Elizabeth from Mount Vernon. She had a "beloved husband," and the promise of a home where she wanted one; and a baby was coming. It gave her joy to think of her grandmother's pleasure in fondling a great-grandchild. A visitor described Nelly in the customary extravagant manner. "I see her the Matron, for such her situation makes her appear, tho' she has been only ten months a wife, lovely as nature could form her, improved in every female accomplishment, and what is still more interesting, amiable and obliging in every department that makes woman most charming, particularly in her conduct to her aged Grand-mother and the General, whom she always called Grand-pa."[35]

November 20, 1799: "Mrs. Summers, Midwife for Mrs. Lewis came here abt. 3 o'clk" Washington wrote in his diary. November 27, 1799: "Doctr. Craik who was sent for to Mrs. Lewis (who was delivered of a daughter abt. ( ) o clock in the forenoon.)" To Bob Lewis Washington wrote, "You will have heard that Nelly Lewis has a girl born." It must have been one of the happiest moments in his eventful, emotion-packed career.

35. Original letter owned by University of Virginia.

"More Friendship Than
Enamoured Love"

A poignant personal note
appeared in a letter from George Washington to Tobias
Lear his first summer of retirement. "I am alone at *present*,
and shall be glad to see you this evening.

"Unless some one pops in, unexpectedly—Mrs. Washington and myself will do what I believe has not been done
within the last twenty years by us,—that is to set down to
dinner by ourselves."

Twenty years and never alone. Two decades of entertaining, war, farming concerns, domestic and foreign
affairs, family demands, and little time for each other. Nelly
remembered that to catch her tall husband's preoccupied
attention, Martha would sometimes stand on tiptoe and
seize one of George's buttons until he looked down on her
and smiled. He was always considerate and tender with his
grandmother, Wash remembered.

Mount Vernon was innundated with guests. From them

come precious descriptions of the first First Family; by this time even Martha was considered worth writing about. She was "cheerful . . . mildness and affability depicted in her countenance . . . said she was no politician, but likes to read the newspapers," wrote one. Washington was often silent with strangers. But his wife put guests at ease with her "free manner that was extremely pleasant and flattering." She "loves to talk and talks very well about times past. She told me she remembered the time when there was only one single carriage in all of Virginia." According to Thomas Jefferson Mrs. Washington was "one of the most estimable of women. . . . [I have] an affectionate and respectful attachment to her."[36]

A woman visitor had respect for her hostess's intellectual capacity. To be sure Mrs. Washington was "incessantly knitting. . . . Her netting too is a great source of amusement. . . . [But] the extensive knowledge she has gained in this general intercourse with persons from all parts of the world has made her a most interesting companion, and having a vastly retentive memory, she presents an entire history of half a century."[37]

With so much company no wonder Washington found "the running off of my cook, has been a most inconvenient thing to this family; and what renders it more disagreeable, is, that I had resolved never to become the master of another Slave by *purchase;* but this resolution I fear I must break." The problem might be alleviated by hiring a housekeeper recommended by nephew Bushrod. "Your Aunts distress for want of a good housekeeper are such as to render the wages demanded by Mrs. Forbes (though unusually high) of no consideration; we must, though very reluctantly, yield to the time she requires to prepare for her fixture here." The housekeeper would have "a warm decent and comfortable room to herself, [and] Victuals from our

36. Thomas Jefferson, *The Writings of Thomas Jefferson*, vol. XIX (Wash., D.C., 1903), p. 130.

37. Original letter owned by University of Virginia.

Table" but must understand that she would "not set at it, at any time *with us.*" "Mrs. Forbes arrived," Washington wrote Bushrod later with relief . . . "gives satisfaction to Mrs. Washington."

Nelly Custis referred to herself in a letter as "deputy housekeeper," but dancing and housekeeping are awkward companions, and Martha still considered her granddaughter somewhat addleheaded. "Keep your feet dry," she had written the eighteen-year-old girl when Nelly was away on a visit and had one of her frequent toothaches. "Take care of your teeth [and] clean them every day. . . . Your brother says he will write you next Sunday," she added. "You know how difficult it is to get him to write." Martha's letter ended with a benediction as characteristic of her as George's letters of avuncular advice are of him. "I hope my dear that this will be a happy year to you and that it will please god to make you good and keep you."

Granddaughters Betsey and Patty were still very much a part of George and Martha's life, even though married and with families of their own. On trips to the federal city the grandparents tactfully divided their time equally between the Peter and Law households. A guest left a charming description of an evening at the Laws' with the Washingtons and Peters. Betsey's ten-month-old daughter came in. "Genl. Washington called to her; he took from his pocket a roll of peach cheese, 'here is something for you' he said and gave her a piece and embraced her."

Fanny and George Augustine's children remained of interest and concern. "My opinion is," Washington wrote Lear, "that you had better, with the least possible delay, get the boys fixed *permanently* at some good school. They will, otherwise, lose precious moments." Fanny Henley, the daughter of Martha's sister Elizabeth, came for a visit and was sent home reluctantly. "Being here a summer or two will carry off all her bilious complaints that she has been so long subject to," Martha wrote her sister.

A wistfulness pervades the retirement correspondence to longtime friends. The distant past is remembered hazily as ideal. To old-flame Sally Fairfax who has moved years ago to England, Washington spoke of "the recollection of those happy moments, the happiest in my life, which I have enjoyed in your company . . . it is a matter of sore regret, when I cast my eyes toward Belvoir which I often do, to reflect that the former Inhabitants of it, with whom we lived in such harmony and friendship, no longer reside there."

Martha wrote Sally in the same vein. "although many years have elapsed since I have either received or written . . . to you, that my affection and regard for you have undergone no diminution, and that it is almost my greatest regrets now that I am again fixed (I hope for life) at this place, at not having you as a neighbour and companion."

"Our circle of friends of course is contracted, without any disposition on our part to enter into *new friendships,* though we have an abundance of acquaintences and a vast variety of Visitors," Martha wrote David Humphreys. Old friend and cousin Lund Washington had died. "His good spirits have never forsaken him a moment under his bodily afflictions," Tobias Lear once wrote. Lear—who had had his own share of afflictions—had returned to Mount Vernon.

The Washington Society of Alexandria sent an invitation to their assemblies. Washington replied regretfully: "Mrs. Washington and myself have been honored with your polite invitation to the Assemblies in Alexandria this winter. . . . But, alas! our dancing days are no more. We wish, however, all those who relish so aggreeable and innocent an amusement, all the pleasure the season will afford them."

When nephew Lawrence Washington became engaged to Miss Mary Wood, he invited his uncle and aunt to the wedding. "I have become engaged to be married to a young lady near Winchester. . . . She has been brought up, in the habit of domestic economy and industry and to consider the true excellence of a farmers wife. . . . Tis unnecessary to add, that I think her withal beautiful and of an amiable disposition."

From Mount Vernon came a gracious but firm no, thank

you. "As wedding Assemblies are better calculated for those who are *coming in to,* than to those who are *going out* of life, you must accept the good wishes of your Aunt and myself in place of personal attendance, for I think it not likely that either of us will ever be more than 25 miles from Mount Vernon again while we are inhabitants of this Terestrial Globe."

Old friend Elizabeth Powel was amused that Martha referred to her husband as "the withered Proprietor" of Mount Vernon. She had also been amused at the discovery of a packet of "love letters" in a secret drawer in the desk she had bought from George when he left Philadelphia and the presidency. "The correspondence [which turned out to be between George and Martha] would, I am persuaded, have been found to be more frought with expressions of friendship than of *enamoured* love," George assured her soberly. He was more light-hearted in asking Mrs. Powel to get Martha a small gift along with a large one for Nelly— "for if a lady felt overlooked, there would be a contest regardless of right—no unusual thing—in which an innocent babe may become the victim of strife."

In the spring of 1799 George wrote Charles's son Samuel, "I am sorry to know that your father has been so much indisposed." The sad news which came in letters from Samuel and nephew-in-law Burgess Ball in September elicited an unusually introspective reply from George. "Your letter . . . has been received informing me of the death of my brother.

"The death of near relations always produces awful and affecting emotions, under whatsoever circumstances it may happen. That of my brother's had been so long expected, and his latter days so uncomfortable to himself, must have prepared all around him for the stroke; though painful in the effect.

"I was the *first,* and am now the *last,* of my fathers Children by the second marriage who remain. When I shall be called upon to follow them, is known only to the giver of life. When the summons comes I shall endeavor to obey it with a good grace.

"Mrs. Washington has been, and still is, very much indisposed, but unites with me in best wishes for you, Mrs. Ball and family. . . ."

Martha was indeed indisposed. George sent for a recipe for a colic remedy one morning, as his wife had had a "distressing night with it." An anguished message went to Thomas Peters ten days later, "if absent, to Mrs. Peters. . . . Mrs. Washington has been exceedingly unwell for more than eight days. . . . Yesterday she was so ill as to keep her in bed all day, and to occasion my sending for Doctor Craik at midnight. She is now better, and taking the Bark; but low, weak and fatigued. . . . Since writing and sealing this letter, Mrs. Washingtons fever has returned with uneasy and restless Symptoms. Inform Mrs. Law thereof."

But it was George who was "called on by the giver of life." December 9, 1799: "Lawrence Lewis and Washington Custis to New Kent," the diary notes. December 12, 1799: "A large circle round the Moon last night. About 10 o'clock it began to snow, soon after to Hail, and then to a settled cold Rain." From ten to three George rode in the harsh weather, and the next day his throat was hoarse. "In the evening the Papers were brought from the Post Office," wrote Lear later, "and he sat in the Parlour, with Mrs. Washington and myself reading them till about nine o'clock when Mrs. W. went up into Mrs. Lewis's room."

George woke Martha between 2 and 3 AM and said he was ill. "She observed that he could scarcely speak and breathed with difficulty, and would have got up to call a Servant; but he would not permit her lest she should take cold."

At dawn Tobias Lear sent immediately for Dr. Craik, and as matters got worse, for two other doctors. Bleeding and other primitive attempts to relieve George's suffering were in vain. He knew he was dying. At 4:30 in the afternoon "he gave his keys to Mrs. Washington and desired her to bring two wills one of them he gave as his true will and desired the other to be burnt, which was done before him."

He instructed Lear to tend to his military records and accounts, asked when Washington Custis and Lawrence

Lewis would return. He gave no reply on hearing that it would not be soon. Lear "wrote a line to Mr. Law and Mr. Peter, requesting them to come with their wives as soon as possible." Confined to her own room with a seventeen-day-old infant was grieving Nelly Custis. "Mrs. Washington was with him all the time, he died in Mr. Lear's arms—When Mrs. Washington asked if all hopes were fled Mr. Lear raised his hand. Mrs. Washington too well construed the token and retired, saying 'My last painful task is over I only wish soon to follow him' he did not take leave of any of the family as he had frequently disapproved of the afflicting farewells which aggravated sorrow on these melancholy occasions."

―――――――

Six months before he died George Washington wrote his "true will," a remarkable document which methodically and sensitively remembered every member of his immediate family.

"To my dearly loved wife Martha Washington [I] give and bequeath the use, profit [an]d benefit of my whole Estate . . . for the term of her natural li[fe] except such parts s[pec]ifically disposed of hereafter." George's slaves were to be freed at the time of Martha's death. (In 1799 the number had increased to 317 for all five farms, 90 at the Mansion House. 14 of those people had been hired from "Mrs. French's.") Nephews George Steptoe and Lawrence Washington were acquitted of debts owed by their estate for education, etc. Martha's sister-in-law Mary Dandridge was made free of the balance of a debt owed by her husband Bartholomew.

Charles Carter, the husband of Betty Lewis's daughter, was assured that certain lots in Fredericksburg were secure, and oldest nephew William Augustine Washington (Austin's son) was offered lots in Richmond and Manchester, if he could use them.

When the will had been written, brother Charles was still alive. To him was given "the gold headed Cane left me by Dr. [Benjamin] Franklin. . . . I add nothing to it, because of the ample provision I have made for his Issue."

To David Stuart, Washington's friend and his daughter-in-law's second husband, Washington left "the large shaving and dressing Table and telescope."

Mourning rings worth one hundred dollars were given ("not for the intrinsic value of them, but as mementos of my esteem and regard") to brother John Augustine's widow, Hannah, and brother Charles's widow, Mildred, to daughter-in-law Eleanor Custis Stuart, and to "my friends" Elizabeth Washington, cousin Lund's widow, and Hannah Washington, wife of first cousin Warner Washington, a frequent visitor to Mount Vernon.

Tobias Lear was given use of the farm he now occupied "free from Rent for life."

To the oldest son of each of Washington's siblings he left one of his swords; they were to choose in the order named, and that order was determined by the age order of their parent: William Augustine Washington (Austin's son), George Lewis (Betty's son; Fielding was older, but apparently still in disgrace with his uncle), George Steptoe Washington (Sam's son), Bushrod Washington (John Augustine's son), Samuel Washington (since George Augustine's death, Charles's oldest son). "These Swords are accompanied with an injunction not to unsheath them for the purpose of shedding blood, except it be for self defence, or in defence of their Country and its rights; and in the latter case, to keep them unsheathed, and prefer falling with them in their hands, to the relinquishment thereof."

After Martha died Mount Vernon was to be divided into three farms. The house itself and surrounding acres were given to nephew Bushrod, son of Washington's favorite brother John Augustine, because "of an old intimation when we [George and John] were Bachelors and he had kindly undertaken to supervise my Estate [Mount Vernon]." Bushrod was also given Washington's papers and library and thus repaid for the years of free legal wo:k he had done for his uncle.

The orphaned sons of George Augustine Washington and Fanny Bassett received one-third of the Mount Vernon estate "in consideration of consanguinity between them and my wife" and "on account of the affection I had for, and the obligation I was under to, their father when living, who from his youth had attached himself to my person, and followed my fortunes through the viscissitudes of the late Revolution; afterwards devoting his time to the Superintendence of my private concerns for many years."

The last third (Dogue Run) was for Nelly Custis and Lawrence Lewis. "It has always been my intention, since my expectation of having Issue has closed, to consider the Grand children of my wife in the same light as I do my own relations, and to act a friendly part by them; more especially by the two whom we have reared from their earliest infancy. . . . Nelly Custis . . . hath lately intermarried with Lawrence Lewis, a son of my deceased Sister Betty Lewis, by which union the inducement to provide for them both has been increased."

George Washington Parke Custis was given a tract of land in Washington and 1000 acres in Alexandria. Wash had already been well provided-for by his Custis inheritance."*

The rest of Washington's estate was to be sold and the proceeds divided into equal parts. Half-brother Austin's children (William Augustine Washington, Elizabeth Spotswood, Jane Thornton and Ann Ashton's heirs) were to receive shares, as were Betty's children (Fielding, George, Robert and Howell Lewis and Betty Carter), Sam's children (George Steptoe and Lawrence Augustine Washington, Harriot Washington Parks, and heirs of Thornton), John Augustine's children (Corbin and the heirs of Jane Washington), and Charles's children (Samuel Washington, Frances Ball, and Mildred Hammond.) Fanny and George Augustine's three children were to divide a share equally, as were Washington's four grandchildren (Elizabeth Parke Law, Martha Parke Peter, Eleanor Parke Lewis, and George Washington Parke Custis) and Bushrod Washington and

*On his land in present-day Arlington, Virginia, Wash built Arlington House, now the Custis-Lee Mansion. (One of his daughters married Robert E. Lee.)

Lawrence Lewis. (Betsey Law and Patty Peter were of course, marred to well-off husbands.)

Executrix and executors of the estate were Martha, nephews William Augustine, Bushrod, George Steptoe, Samuel, and Lawrence, and Wash (when he reached twenty). The will was dated "in the year one thousand seven hundred and ninety-nine and of the Independence of the United States the twenty-fourth." Bequests were made to further the education of the poor and of potential leaders of those United States to whom so much had already been given by George Washington. To the end the intricate strands of his celebrated life were woven together. As he provided for his family, he remembered his country, just as during the demanding years of public service family members' needs and an ingrained, deeply felt affection for them permeated his consciousness.

"Best affections to my Sister and the little ones."

"My love and best wishes attend my sister and every part and parcel of your family."

"Your aunt joins me in love to you all."

"God grant you all health and happiness; nothing in this world would contribute so much to mine as to be once more fixed among you in the peaceable enjoyment of my own Vine, and fig Tree."

Yr.

Geo. Washington

AFTERWORD

"I only wish soon to follow him," Martha told Tobias Lear when George died. Two years later she lay beside her husband in the old family vault. (Both graves were subsequently moved to a larger, more pretentious tomb.)

Nelly, Lawrence, and their babies had lived with Martha at Mount Vernon until her death; soon afterward they moved to Woodlawn, the handsome house they had built on the nearby Dogue Run land left them by Washington. Patty and Thomas Peter raised their family in the new capital at Tudor Place, which until recently was lived in by their descendants.

Not surprisingly, Betsey and Thomas Law's marriage barely survived her grandparents' lifetimes. After Martha's death, Betsey shocked Washington society by divorcing her husband; he was given custody of their only child. Betsey was "the victim of slander and persecution," she wrote a male friend who "once vowed to love me forever." But slander and persecution did not daunt her spirit. Betsey set her cap for the French minister, according to Dolley Madison, and "gave her hand" to the bogus Count de Crillon of Spain. "He vows he never asked for it," gossiped Dolley.

George Washington Parke Custis—the child "as full of spirits as an eggshell is of meat," the "moped and Stupid" adolescent "always in some hole or corner excluded from

Company"—became a responsible and likable adult devoted to honoring his step-grandfather's memory.

Bushrod and Nancy Washington who had no children of their own, left Mount Vernon to his brother Corbin's son, John Augustine Washington 2nd. He left the mansion to his son, John Augustine Washington 3rd, who sold it to the Mount Vernon Ladies' Association in 1858.

Mount Vernon, Woodlawn, the Custis-Lee Mansion, Washington's childhood home Wakefield, Betty's Kenmore, and Mary Washington's house in Fredericksburg are open to the public; in time Tudor Place may be. A new building for the Mount Vernon Library is currently under construction in one of George Washington's fields with a fine view of the Potomac River. "No estate in United America is more pleasantly situated than Mount Vernon," claimed its proprietor—especially with Martha.

> "I should enjoy more real happiness in one month with you at home, than I have the most distant prospect of finding abroad, if my stay were to be seven times seven years."
>
> GEORGE WASHINGTON TO MARTHA WASHINGTON, JUNE 18, 1775

Index of Relatives

BIBLIOGRAPHY

Adams, Abigail. *New Letters of Abigail Adams, 1788–1801.* Edited by Stewart Mitchell. Boston, 1947, 1971.

Adams Family Correspondence. Edited by L. H. Butterfield. Cambridge, 1963.

Adams, John. *Diary and Autobiography of John Adams.* Edited by L. H. Butterfield. Vol. 3. Cambridge, 1961.

———. *Letters of John Adams Addressed to His Wife II.* Boston, 1841.

Custis, George Washington Parke. *Recollections & Private Memoirs of Washington.* Edited by Benson J. Lossing. Philadelphia, 1860.

Decatur, Stephen, Jr. *Private Affairs of George Washington.* Boston, 1833.

Fithian, Philip Vickers. *Journal and Letters, 1767–1774.* Princeton, 1900.

Flexner, James Thomas. *George Washington.* 4 vols. Boston and Toronto, 1965–1969.

———. *Traitor and Spy.* Boston, 1953.

Freeman, Douglas Southall. *George Washington.* 7 vols. New York, 1948–1951.

Hamilton, Stanislaus Murray, ed. *Letters to Washington and Accompanying Papers.* 5 vols. Boston and New York, 1898–1902.

Irving, Washington. *Life of George Washington.* Vol. V. New York, 1859.

Jefferson, Thomas. *The Writings of Thomas Jefferson.* Vol. XIX. Washington, 1903.

Latrobe, Benjamin. *Journal.* New York, 1905.

Lear, Tobias. *Letters and Recollections of George Washington.* London, 1906.

Moore, Charles. *The Family Life of George Washington.* Boston and New York, 1926.

Mount Vernon Ladies' Association Manuscript Collection.

Muir, Dorothy Troth. *General Washington's Headquarters,* 1775–1783. Troy, Ala., 1977.

Niemcewicz, Julian Ursyn. *Under Their Vine and Fig Tree: Travels through America.* Elizabeth, N.J., 1965.

Sipe, C. Hale. *Mount Vernon and the Washington Family.* Butler, Pa., 1929.

Thane, Elswyth. *Mount Vernon Family.* New York, 1968.

———. *Potomac Squire.* New York, 1963.

———. *Washington's Lady.* New York, 1954.

Washington, George. *Diaries.* Edited by John C. Fitzpatrick. 4 vols. Boston and New York, 1925.

———. *The Diaries of George Washington.* Edited by Donald Jackson. 4 vols. Charlottesville, Va., 1976, 1978.

———. *Writings.* Edited by John C. Fitzpatrick. 39 vols. Washington, 1931–1944.

Wayland, John W. *The Washingtons and Their Homes.* Staunton, Va., 1944.